SONIC™

THE HEDGEHOG

THE OFFICIAL
COLORING BOOK FOR ADULTS

INSIGHT EDITIONS

SAN RAFAEL • LOS ANGELES • LONDON

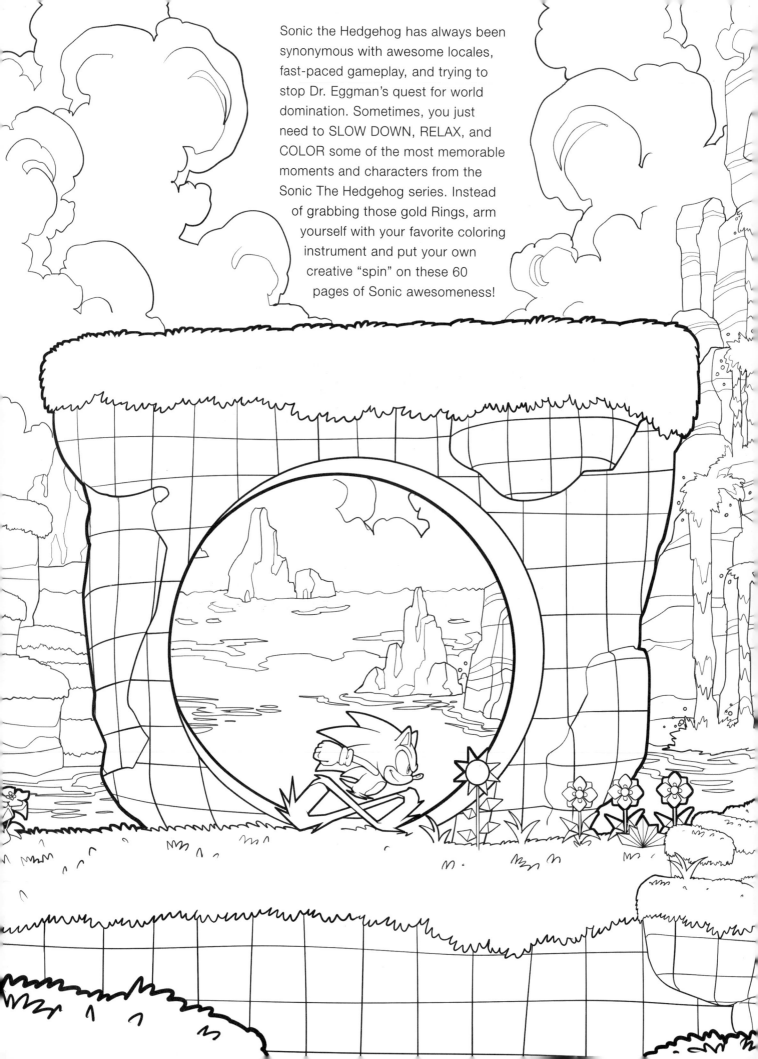

Sonic the Hedgehog has always been synonymous with awesome locales, fast-paced gameplay, and trying to stop Dr. Eggman's quest for world domination. Sometimes, you just need to SLOW DOWN, RELAX, and COLOR some of the most memorable moments and characters from the Sonic The Hedgehog series. Instead of grabbing those gold Rings, arm yourself with your favorite coloring instrument and put your own creative "spin" on these 60 pages of Sonic awesomeness!

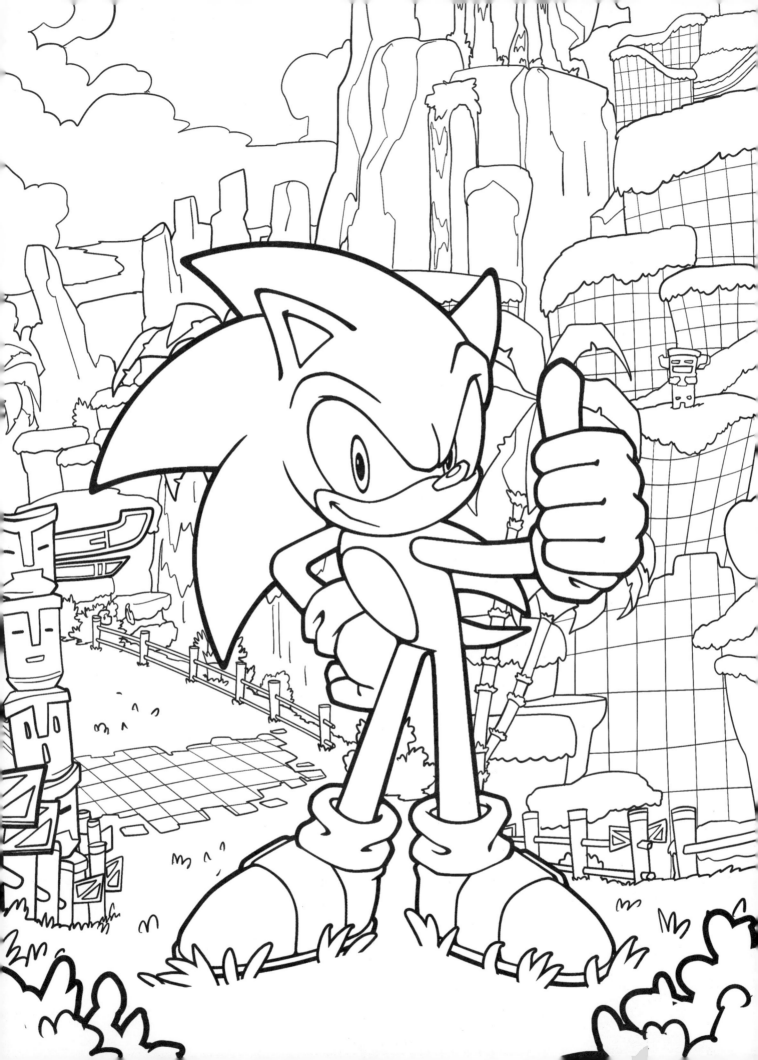

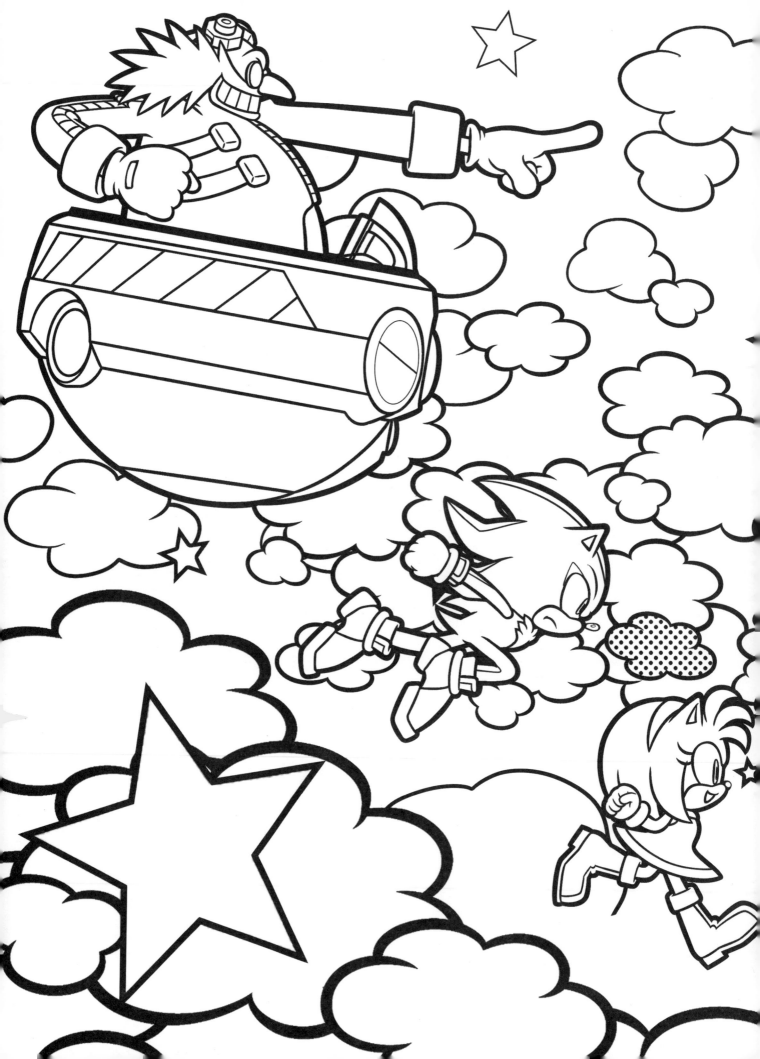

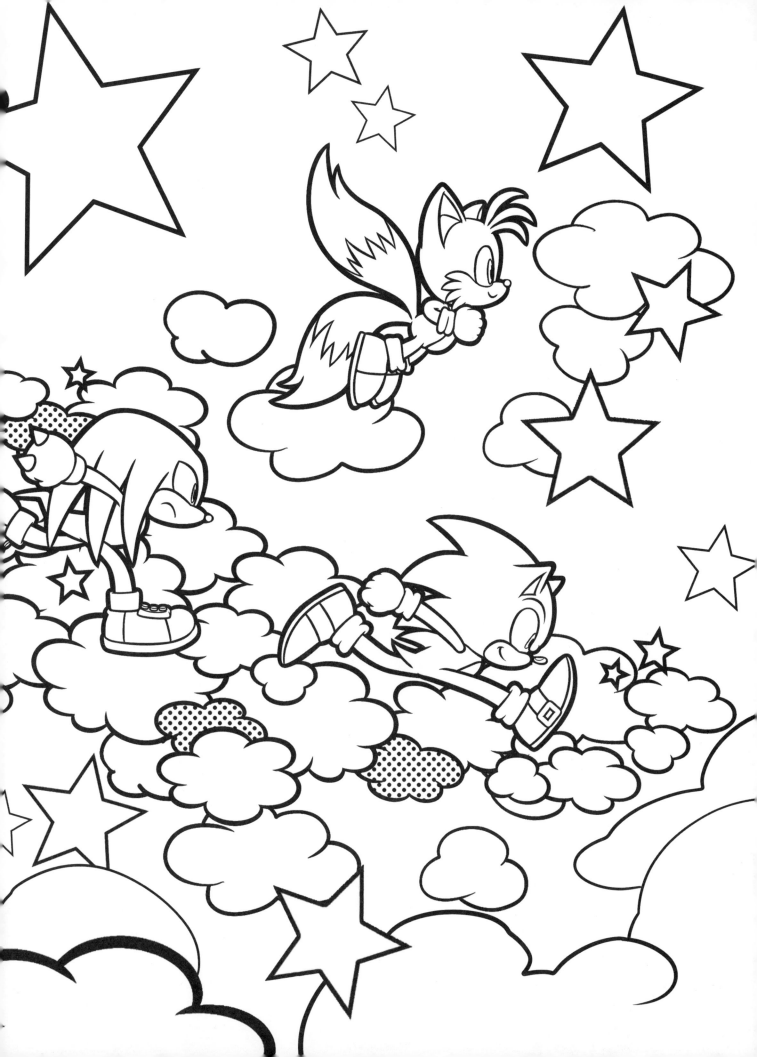

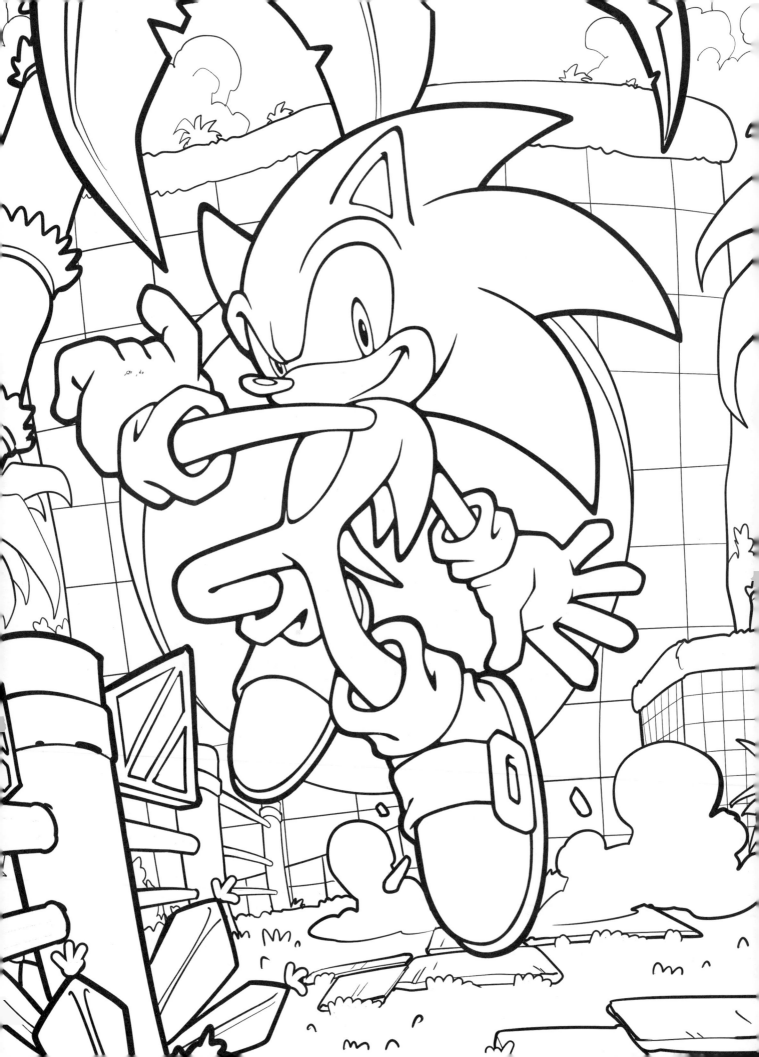

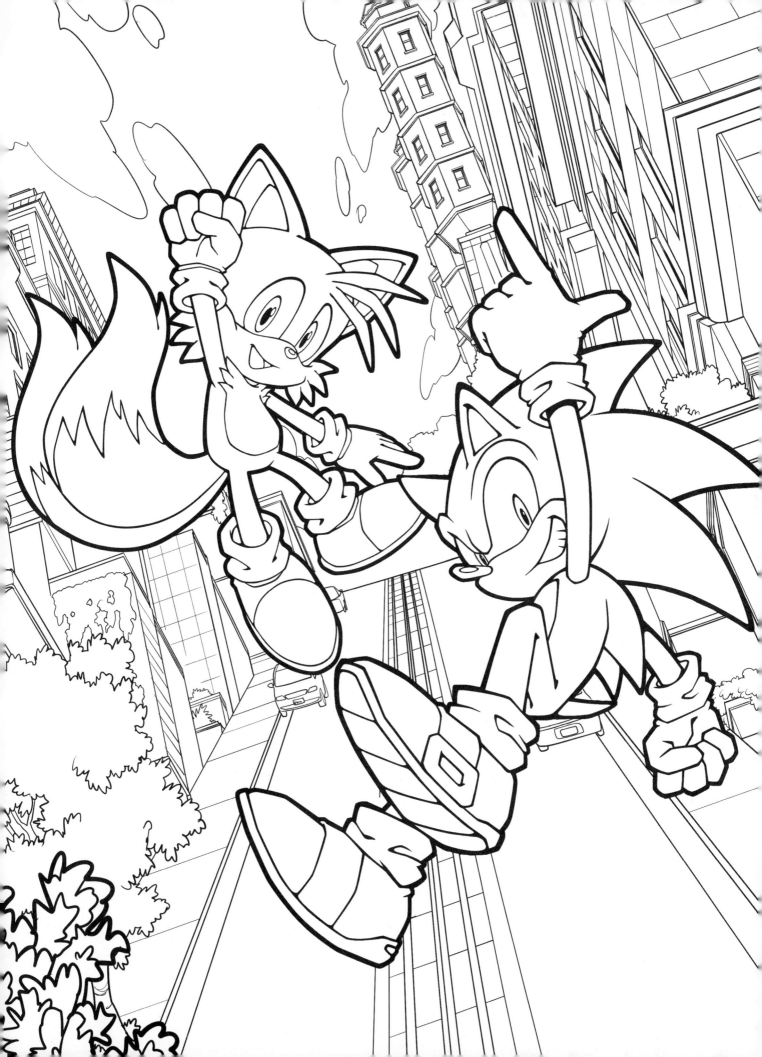

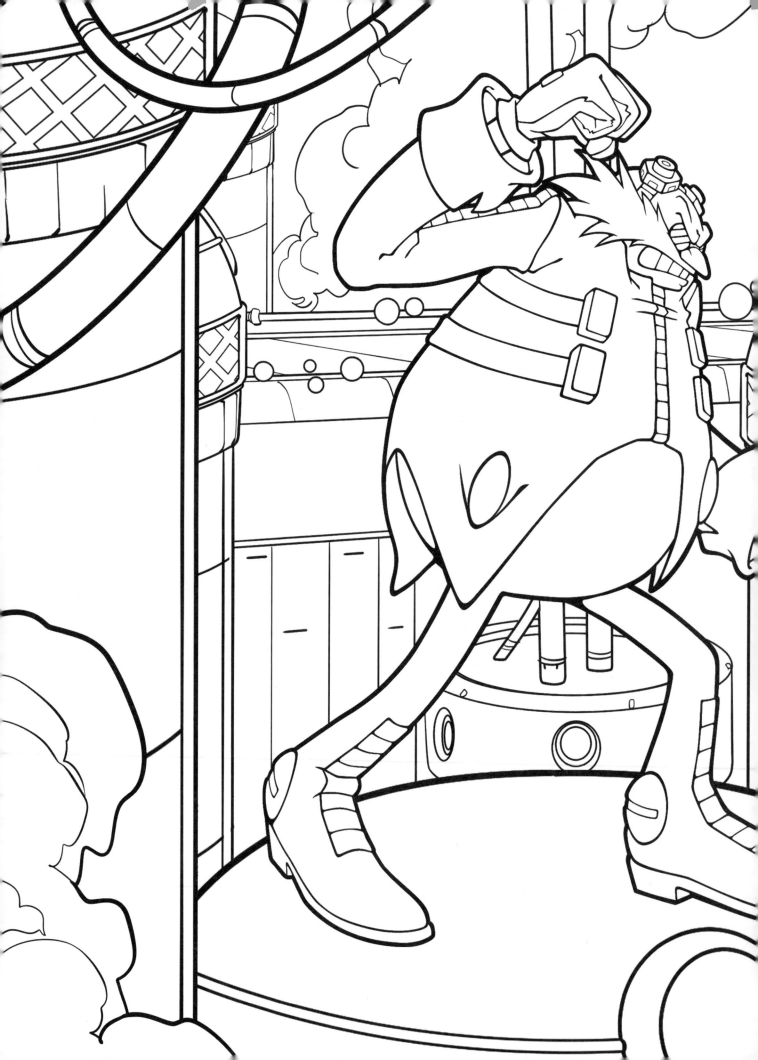

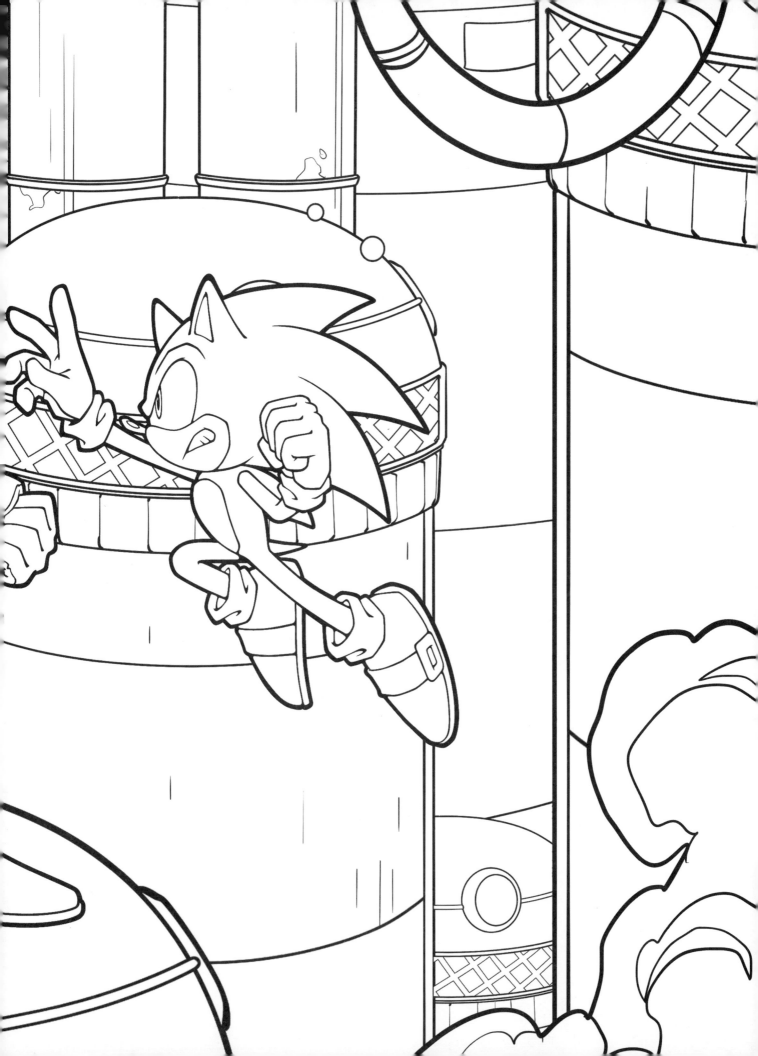

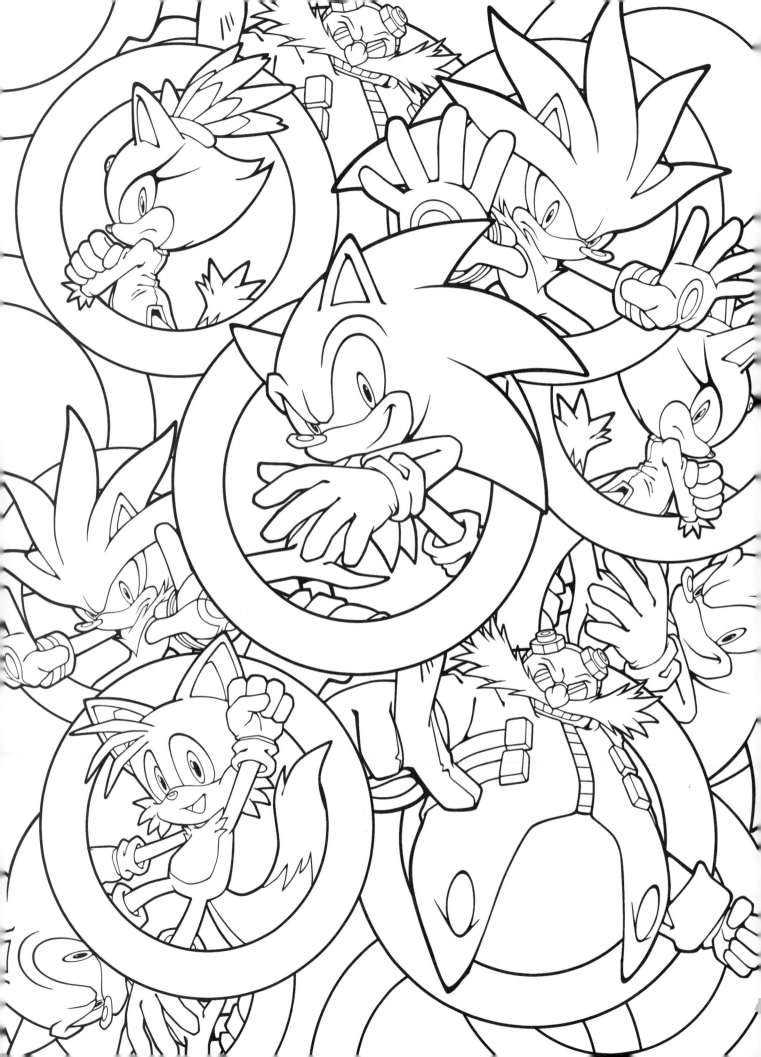

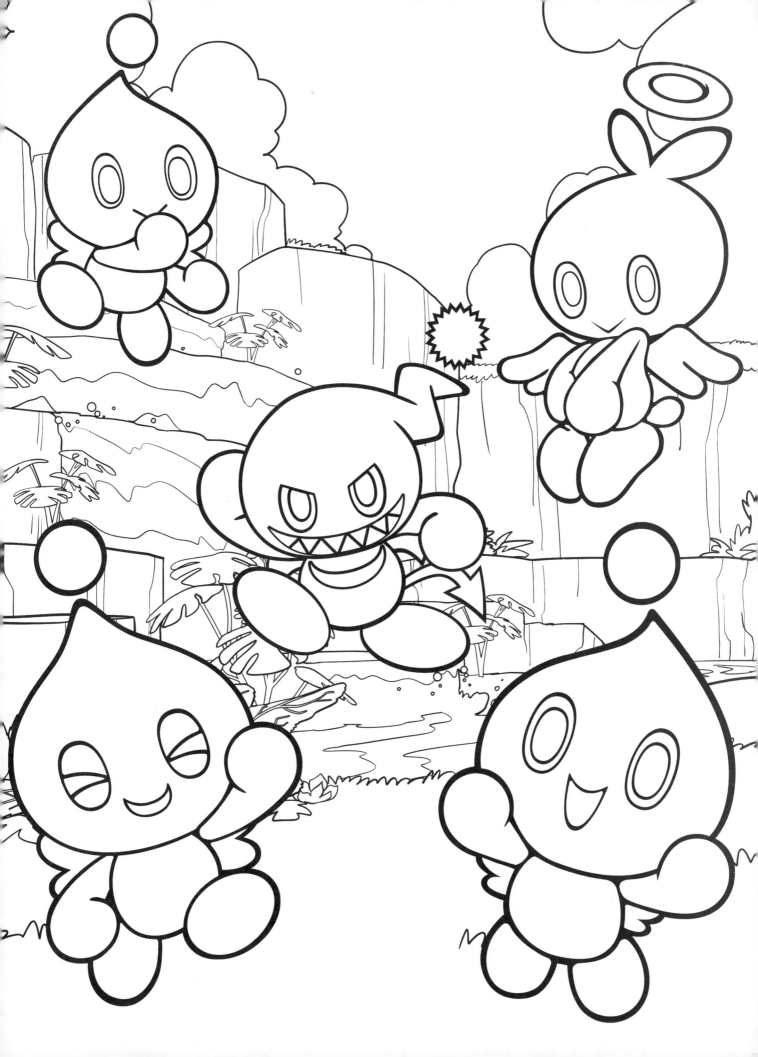

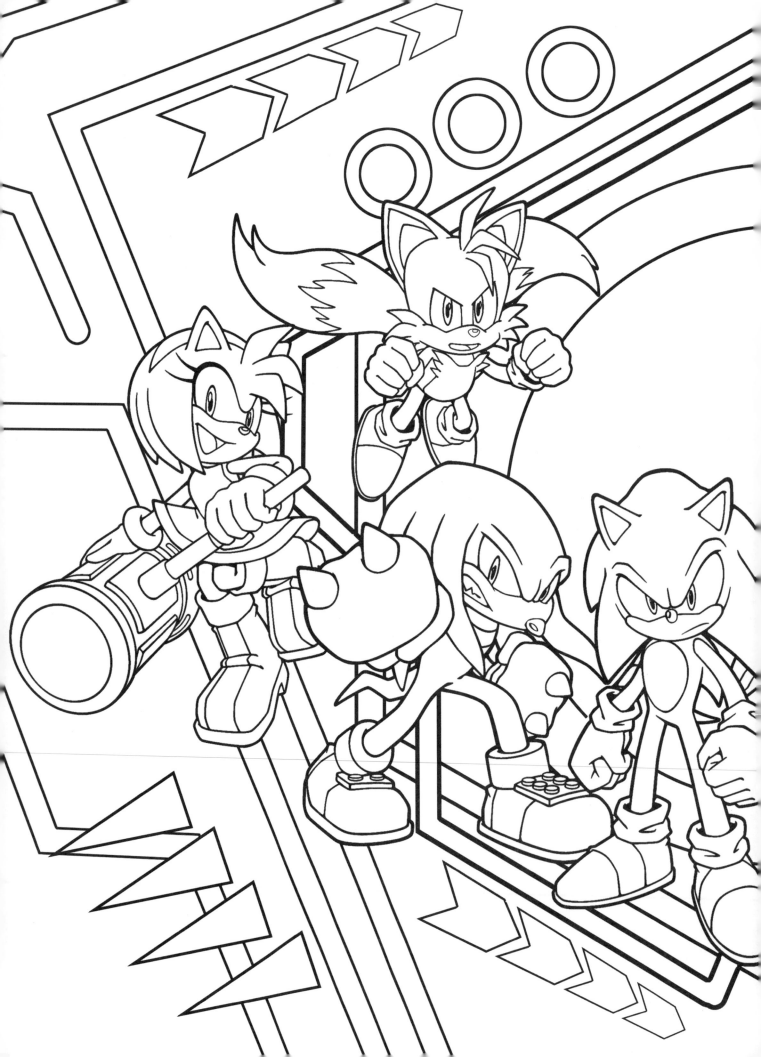

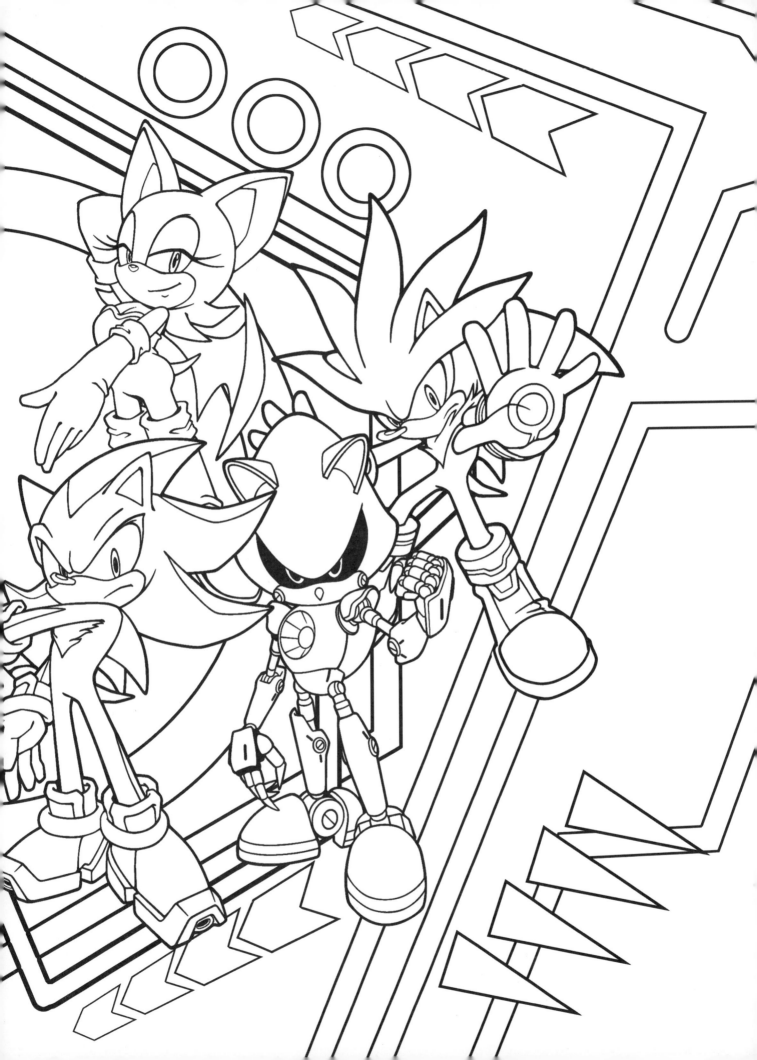

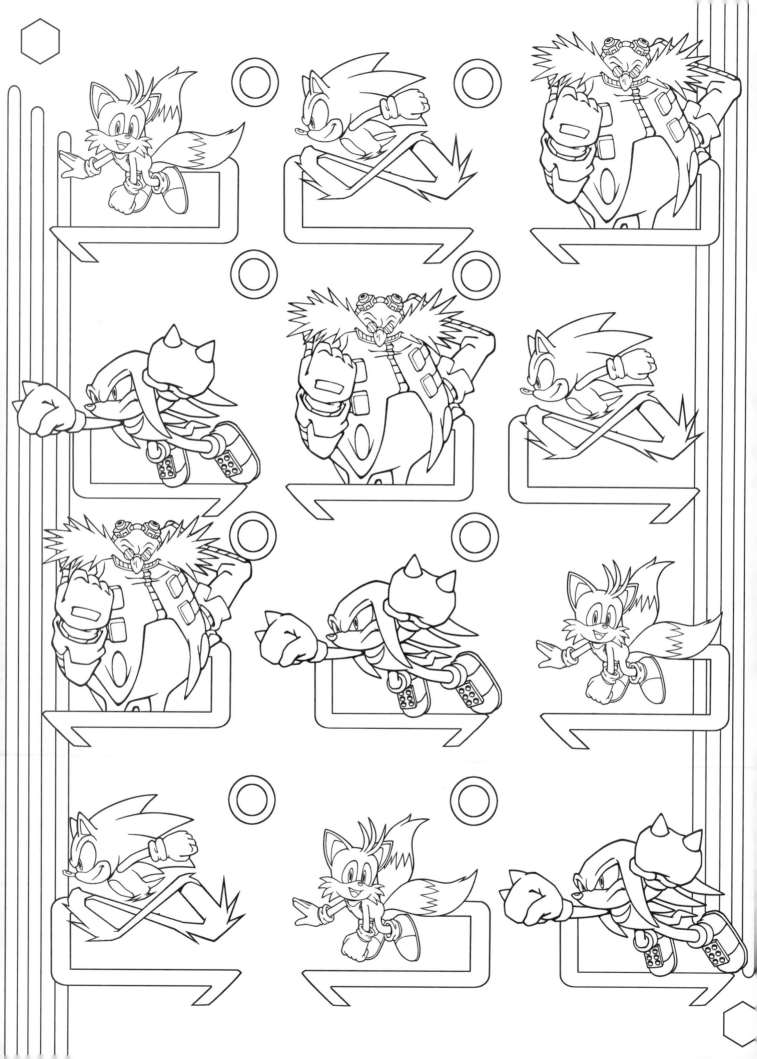

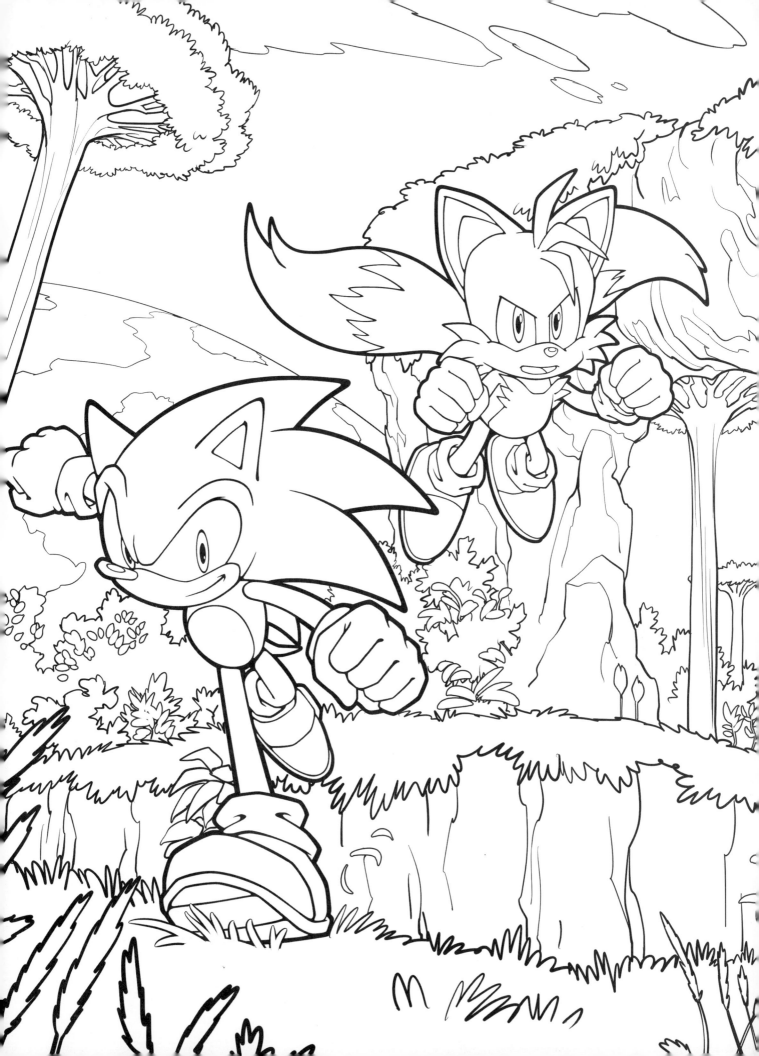

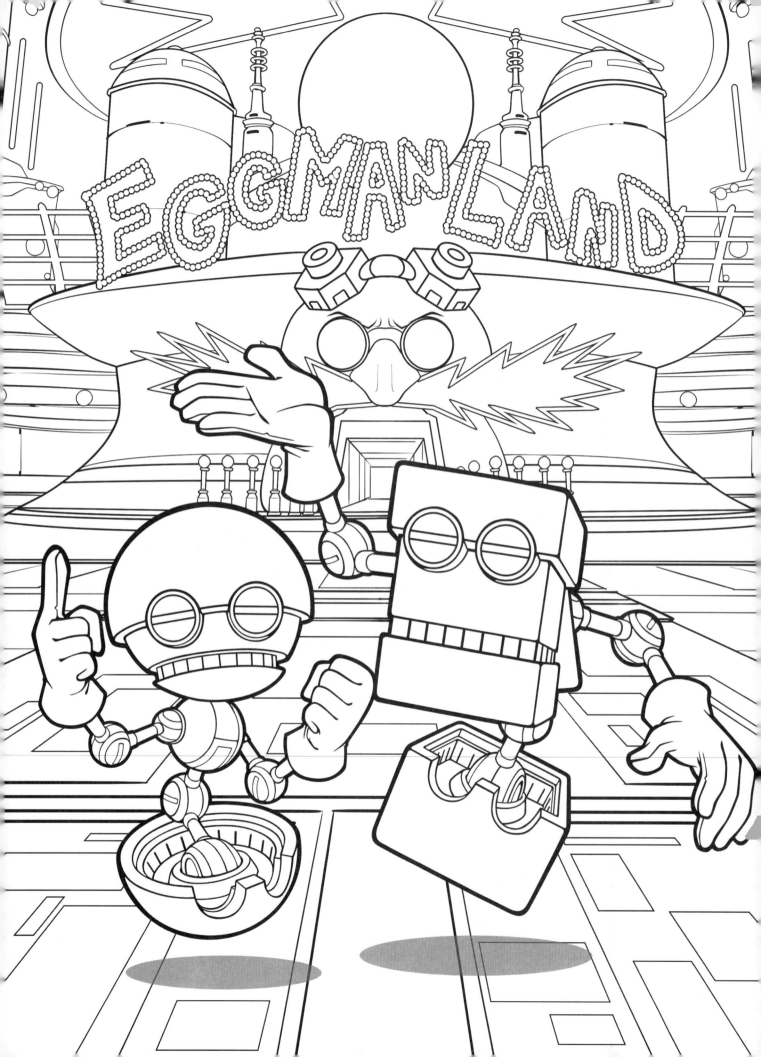

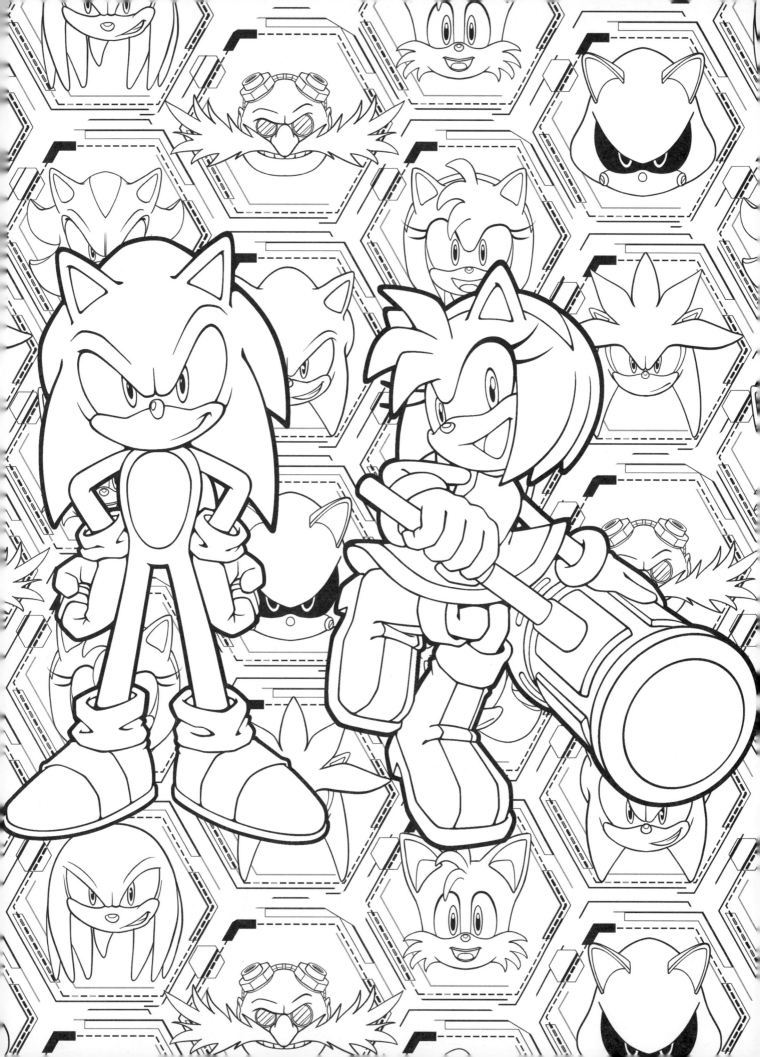

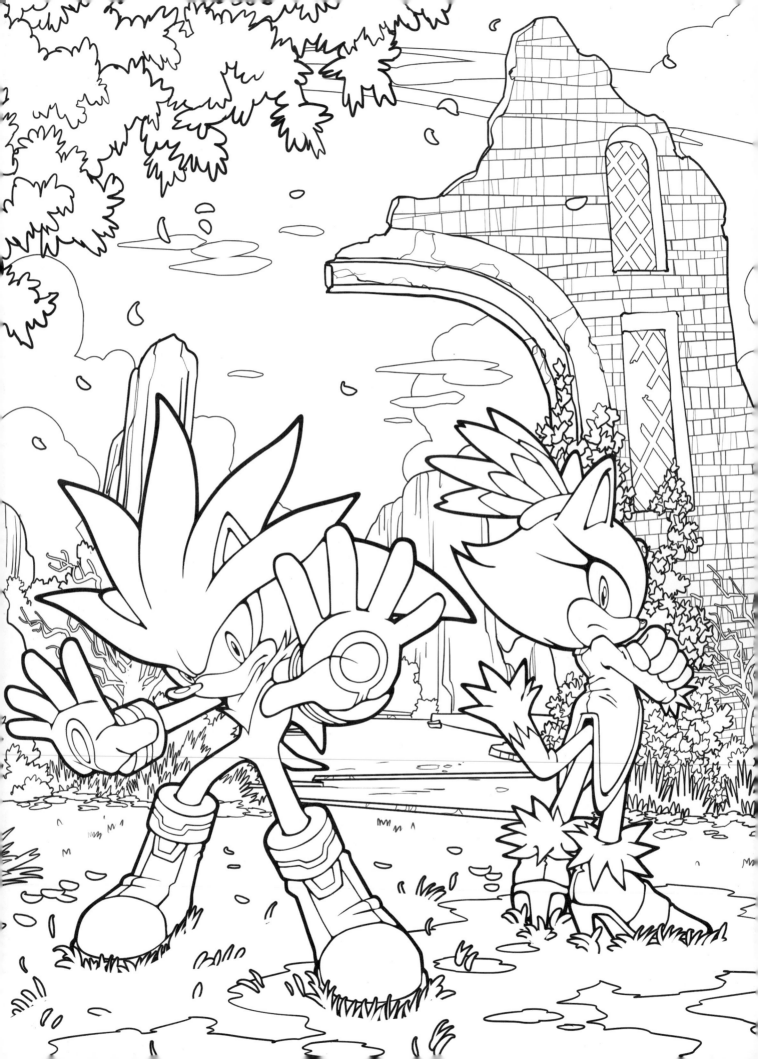

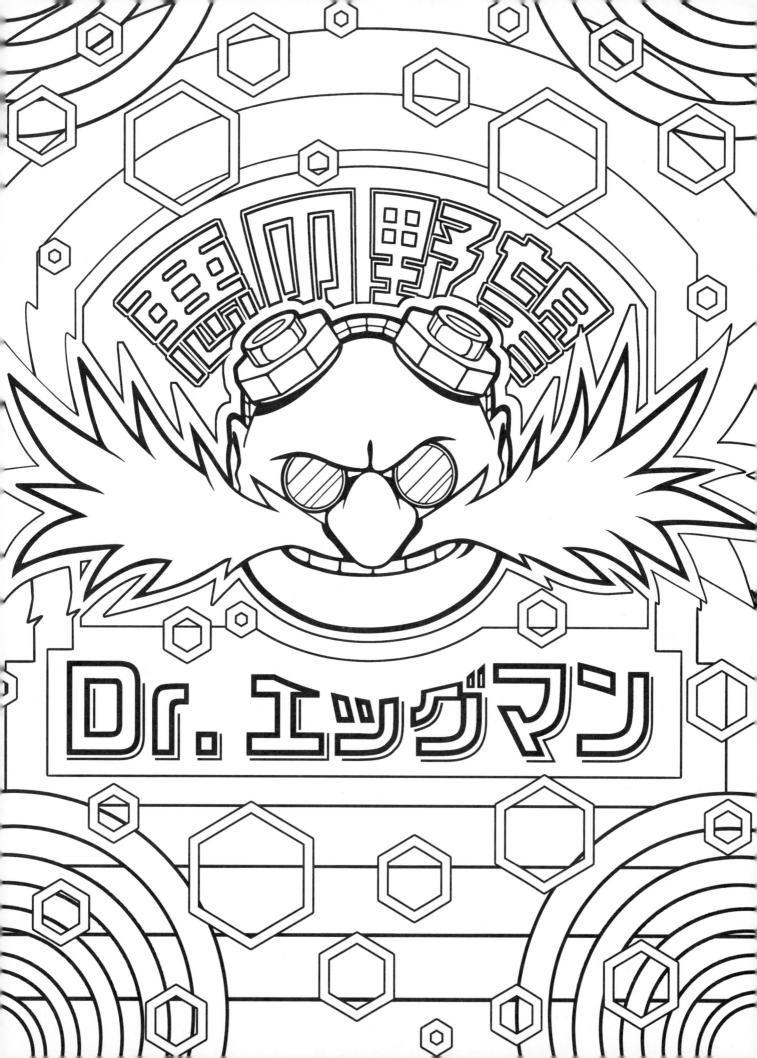

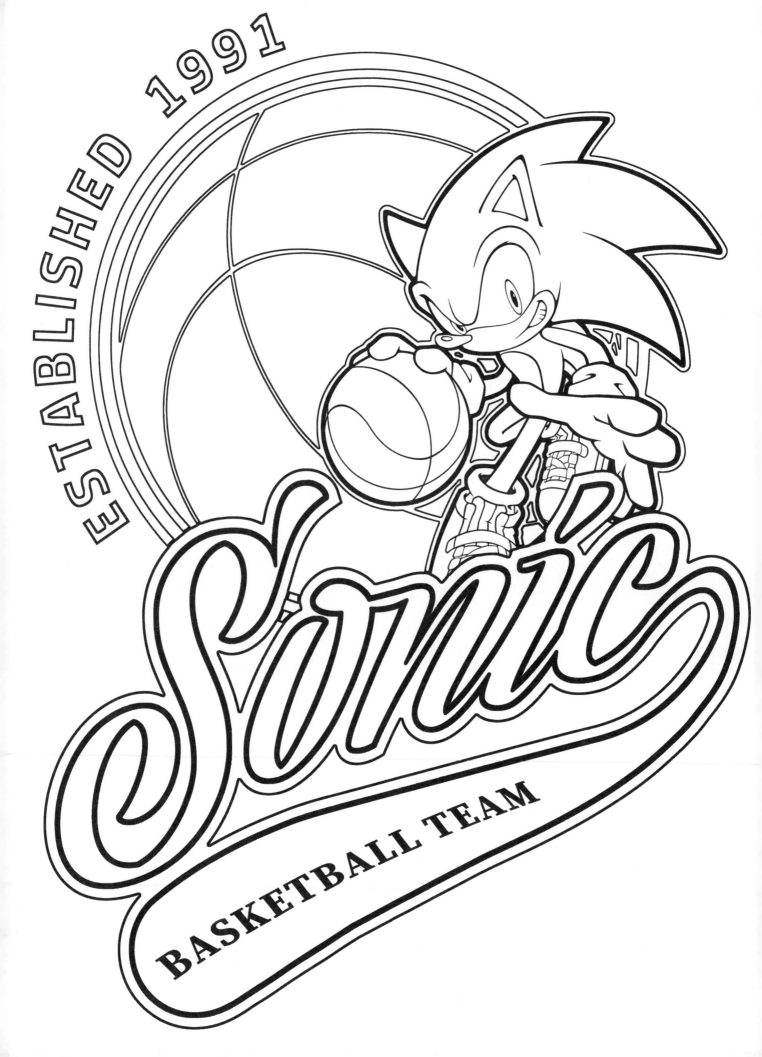

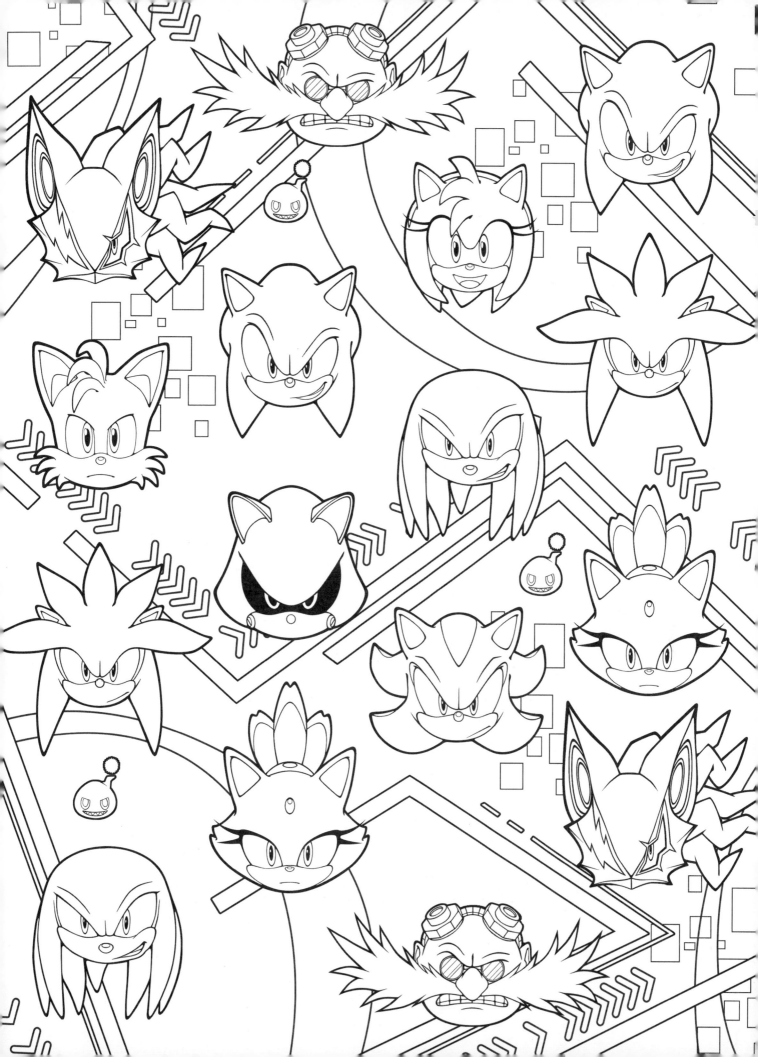

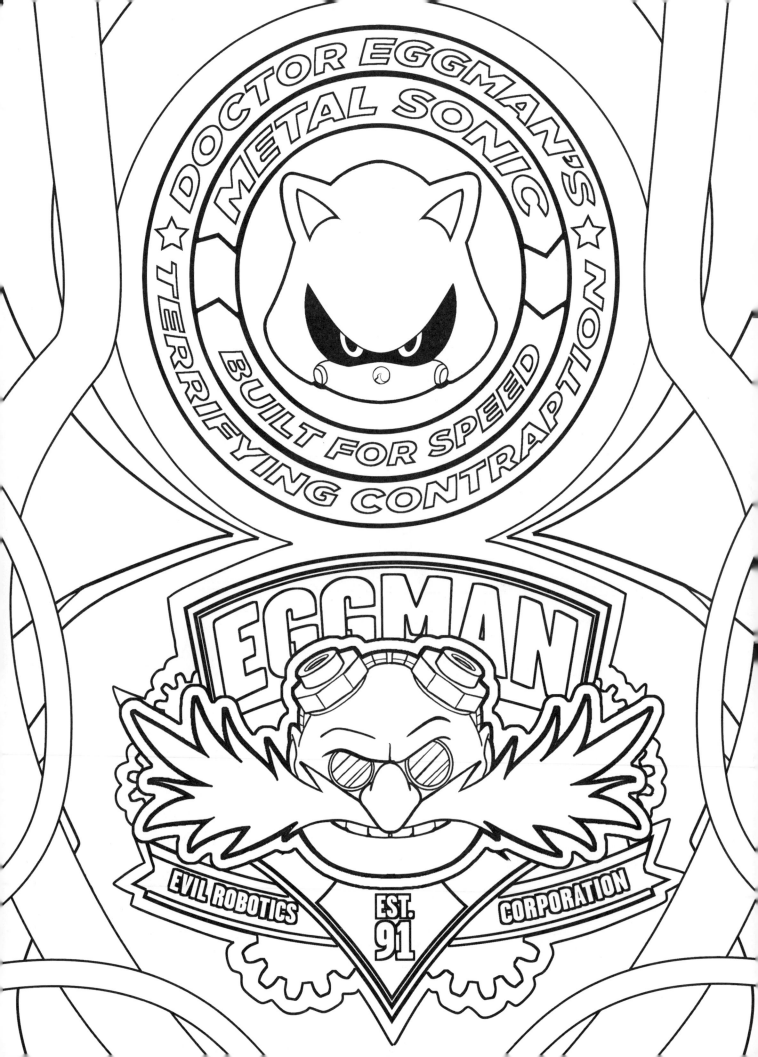

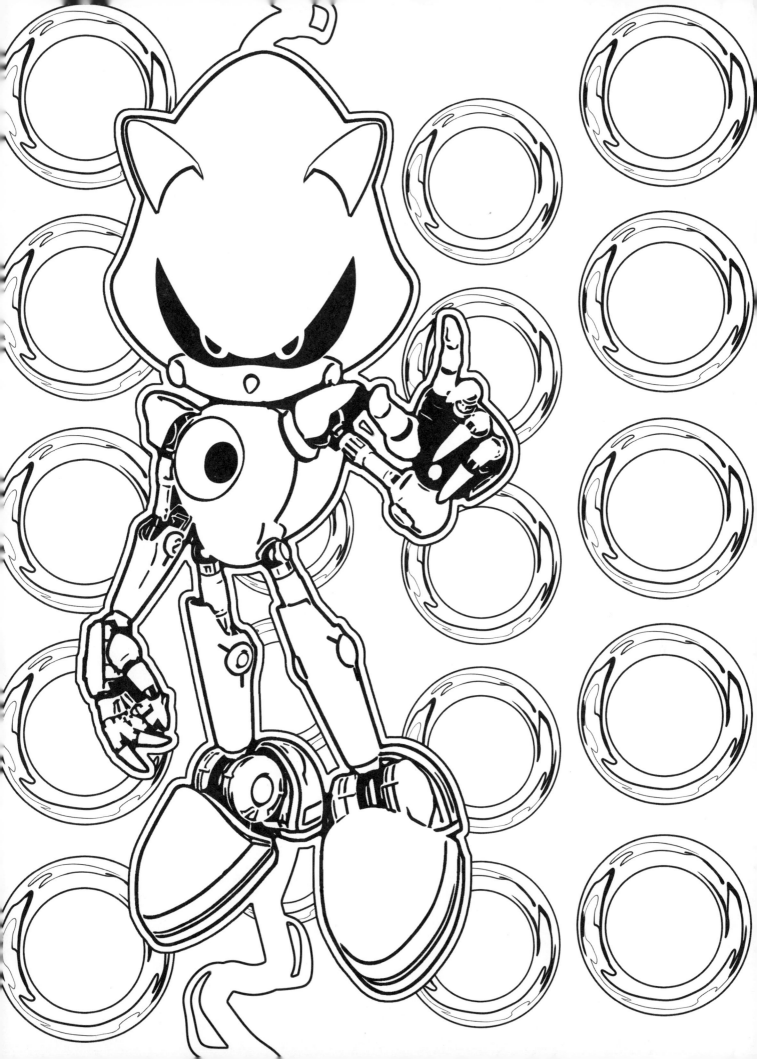

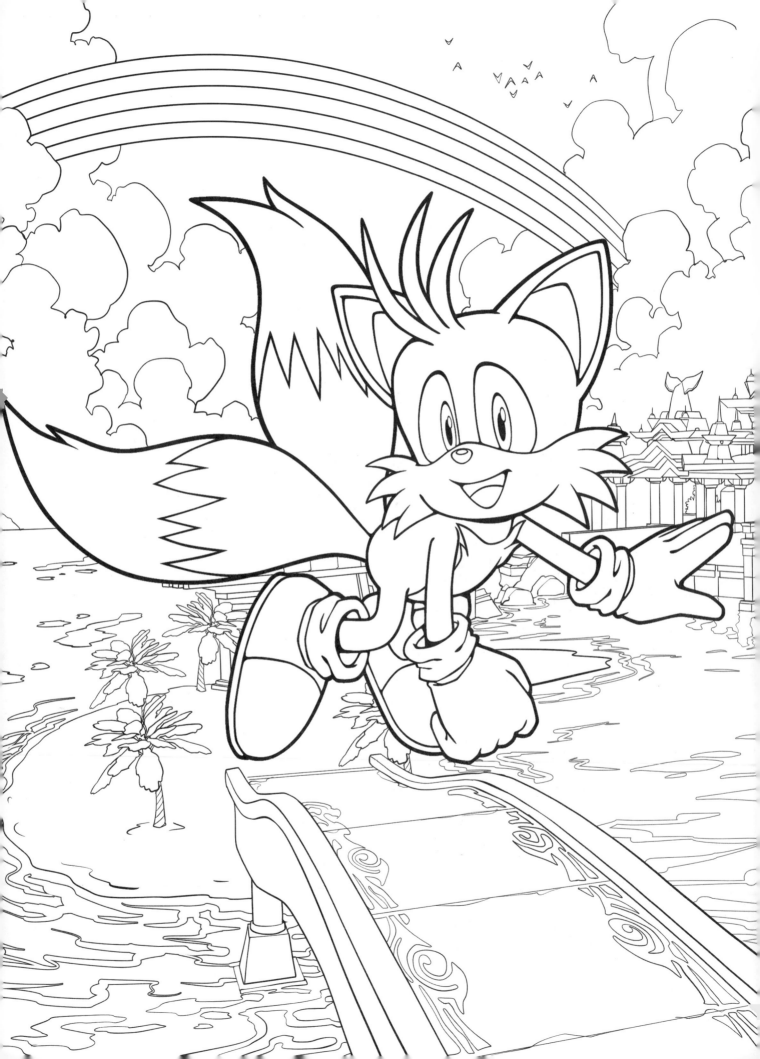

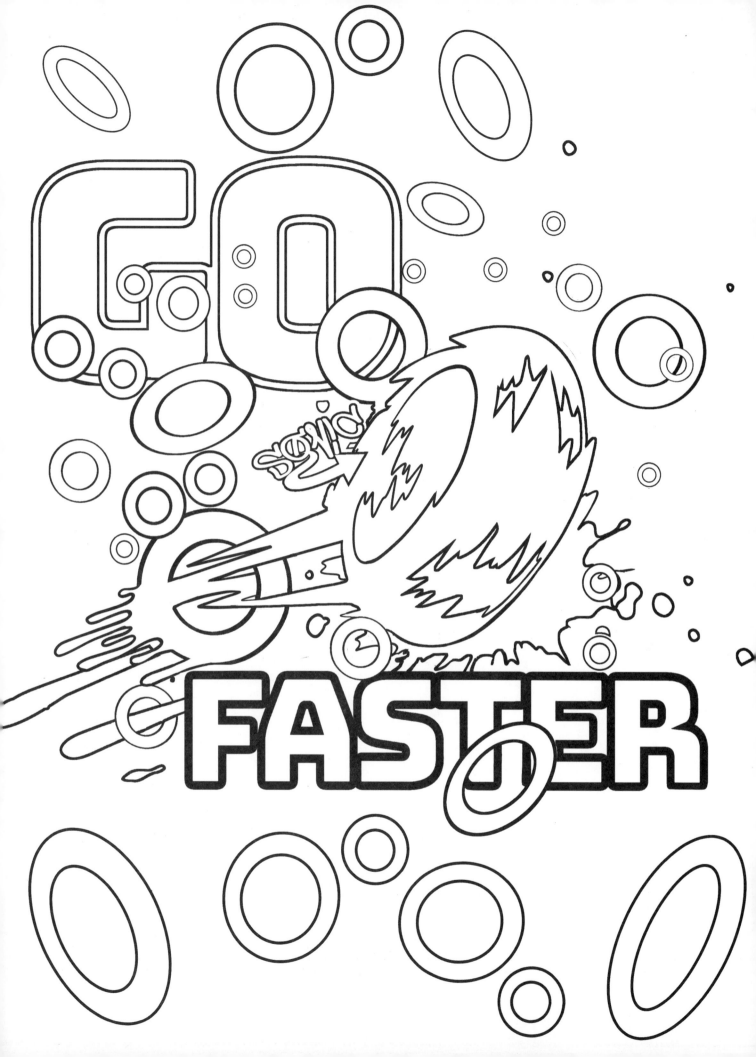

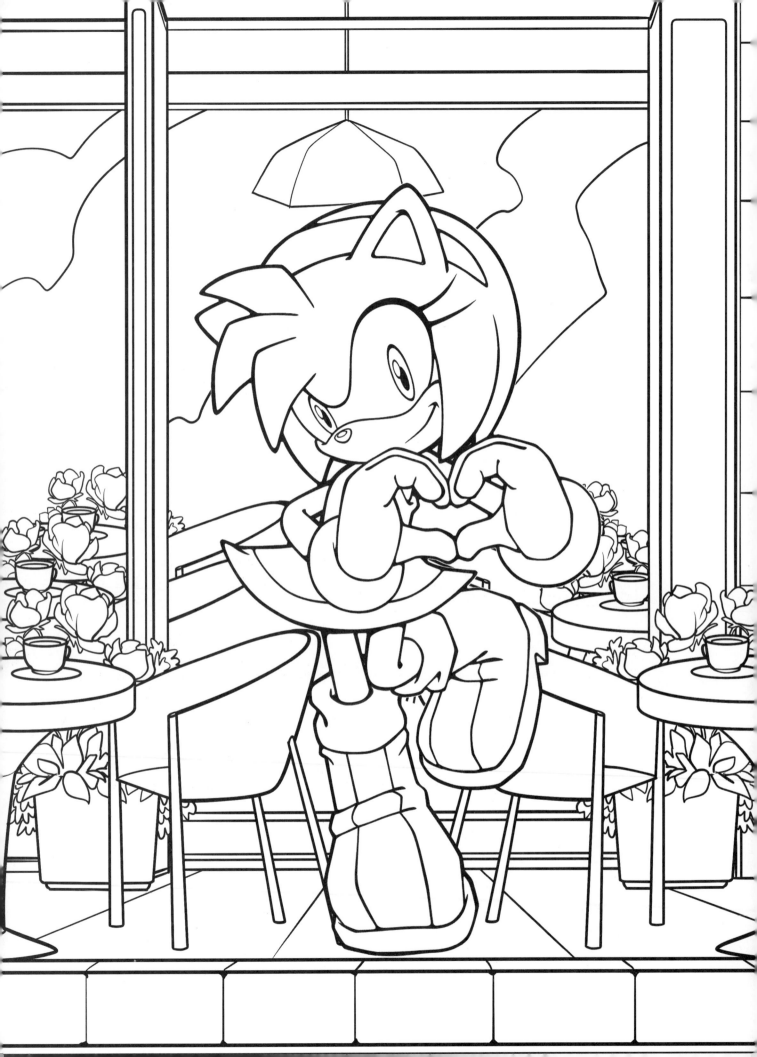

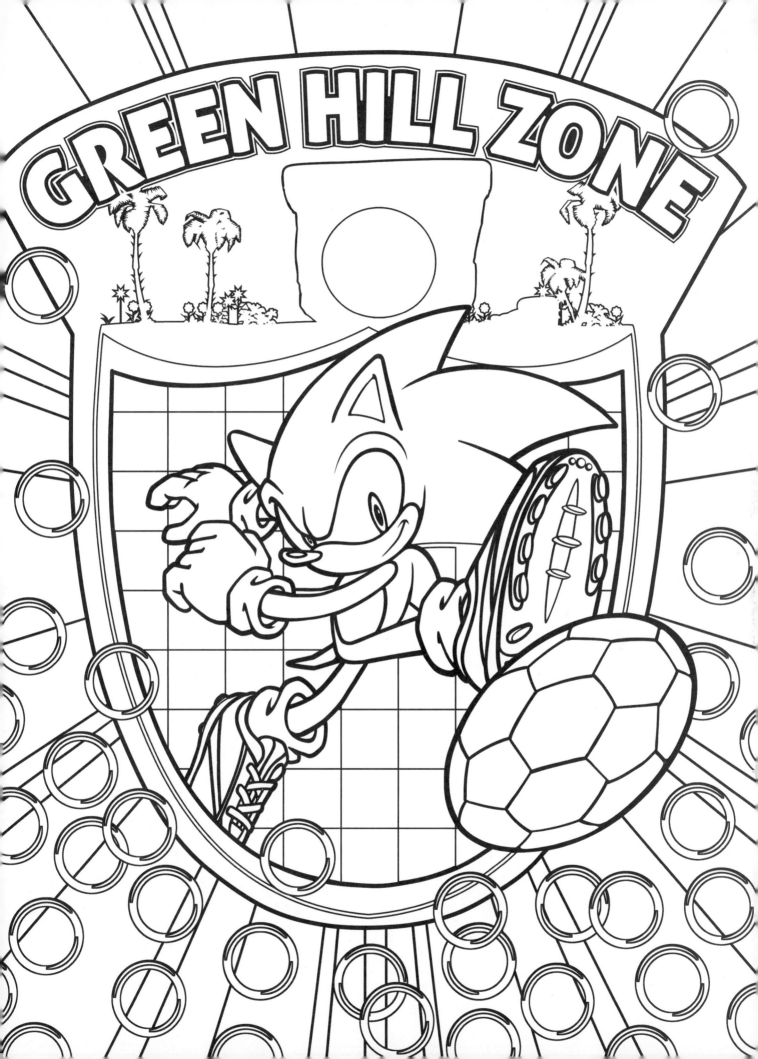

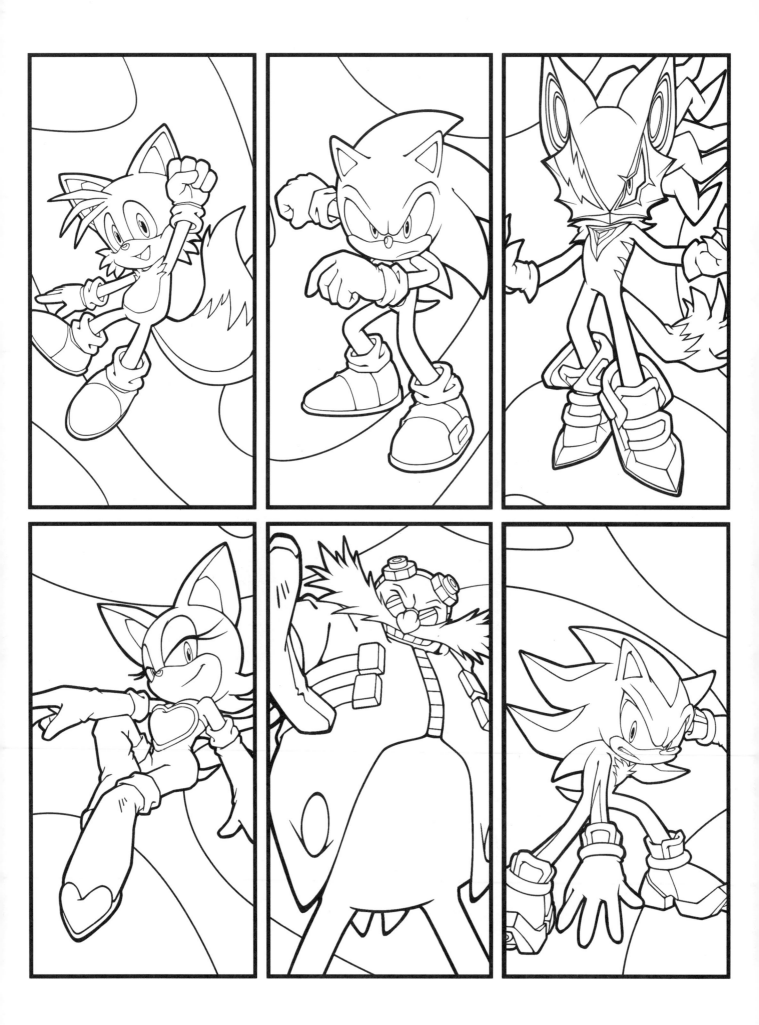

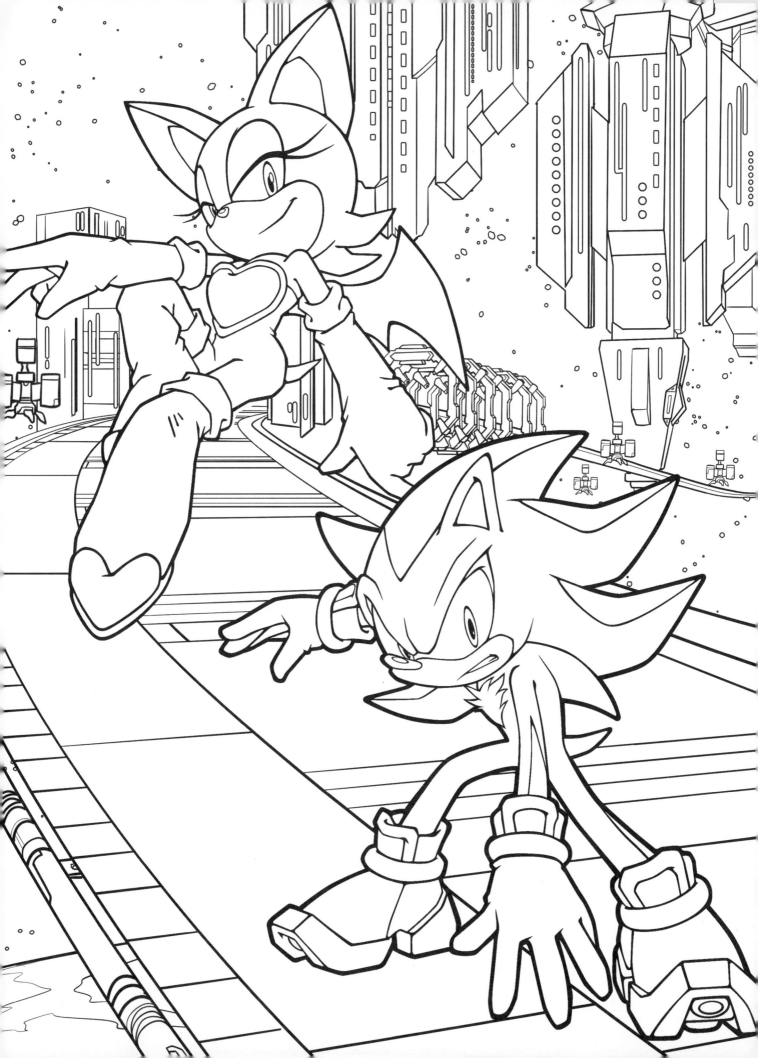

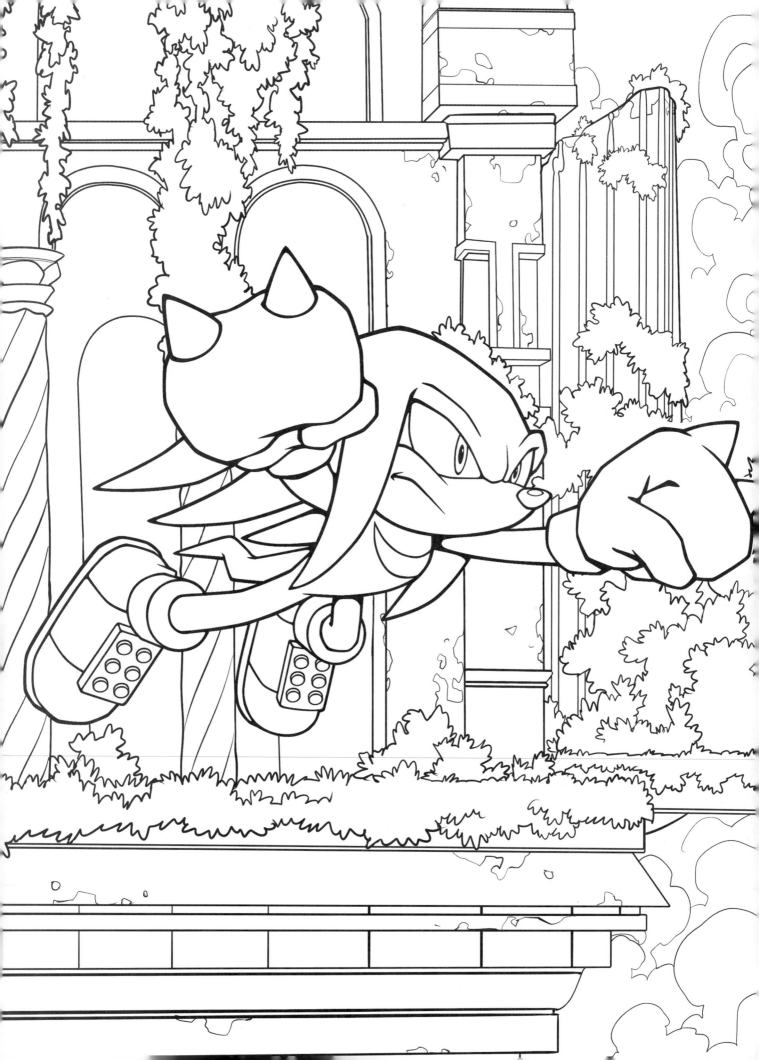

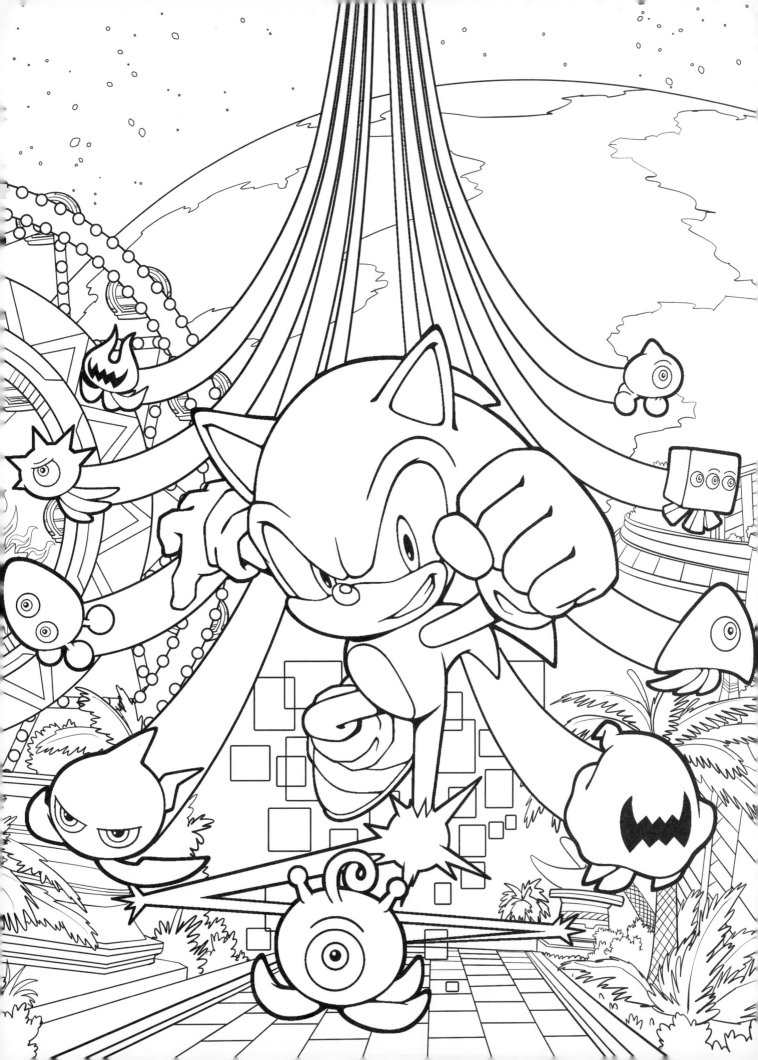

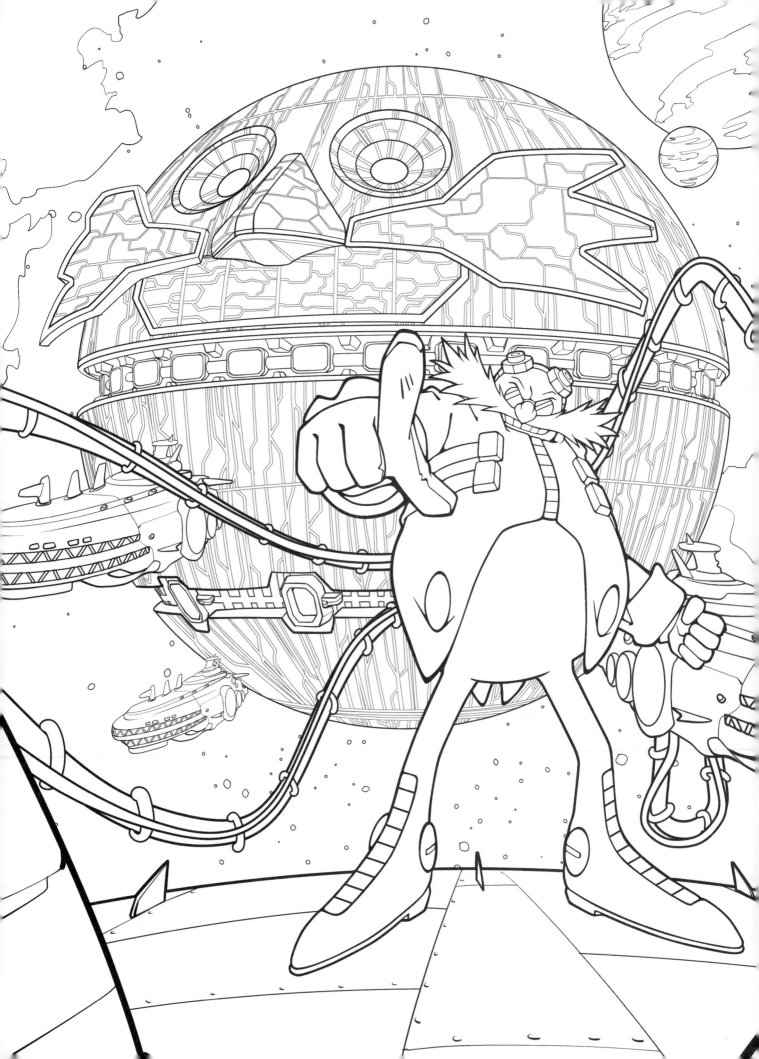

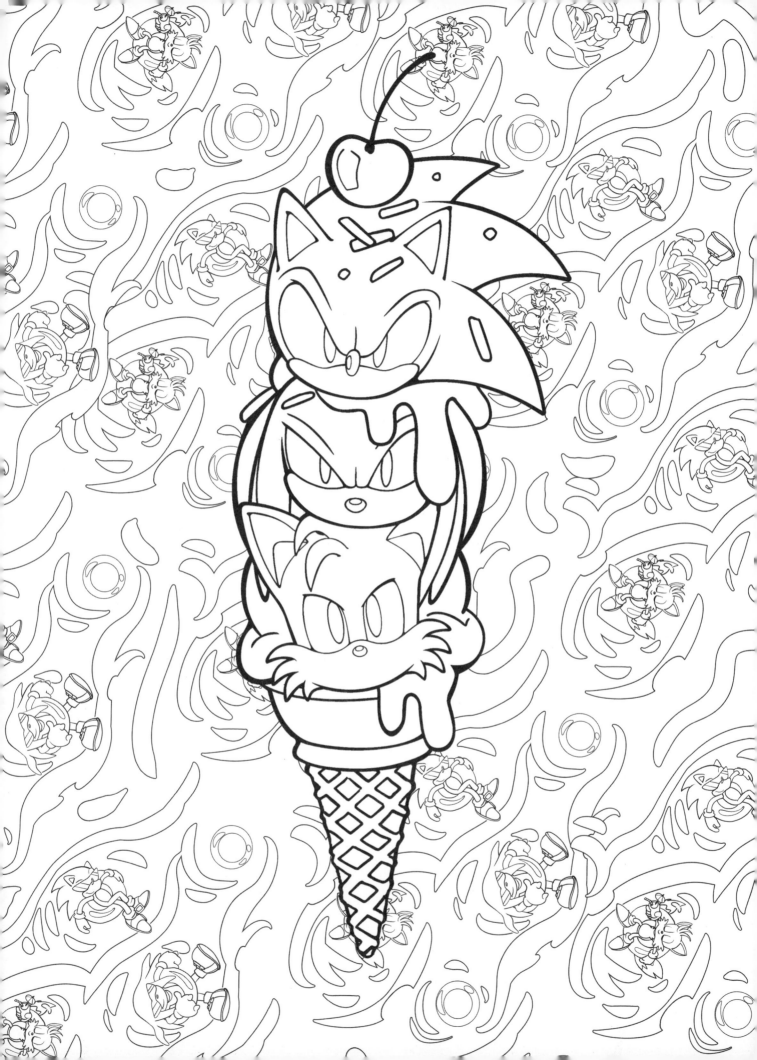

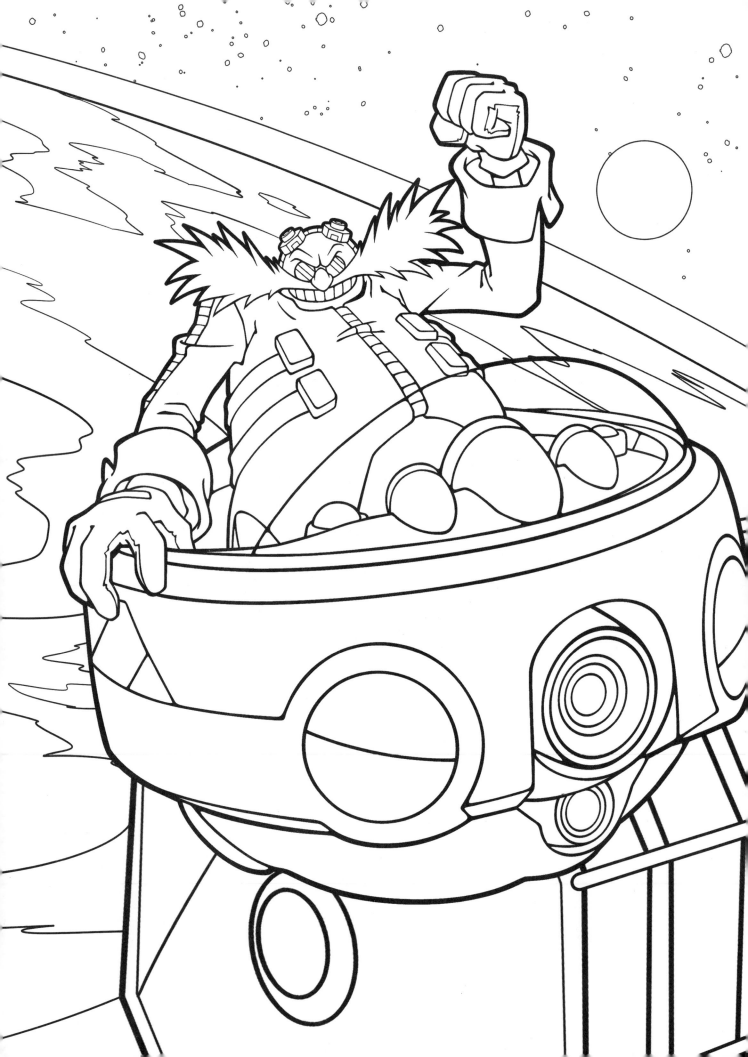

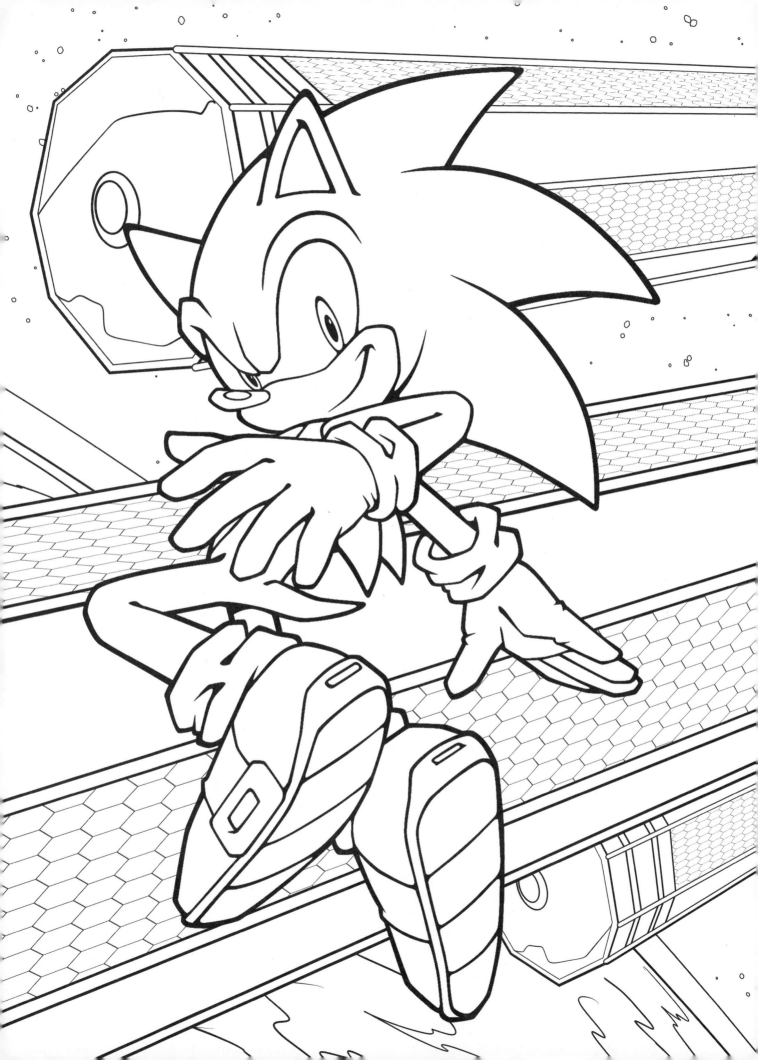

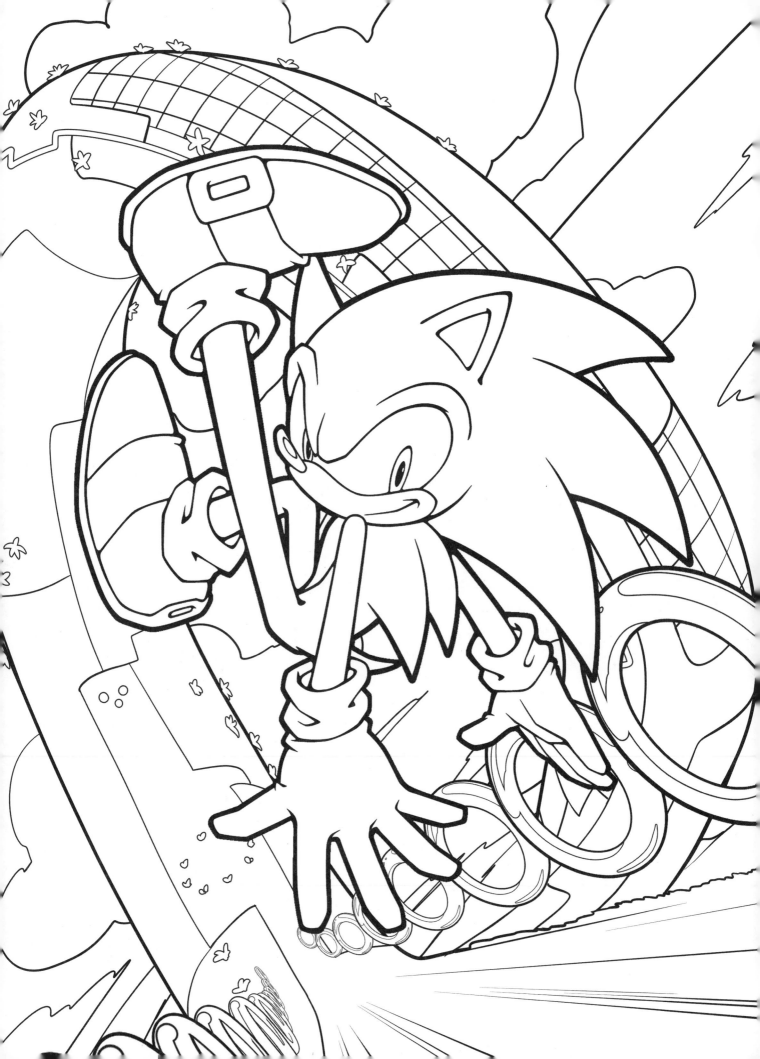

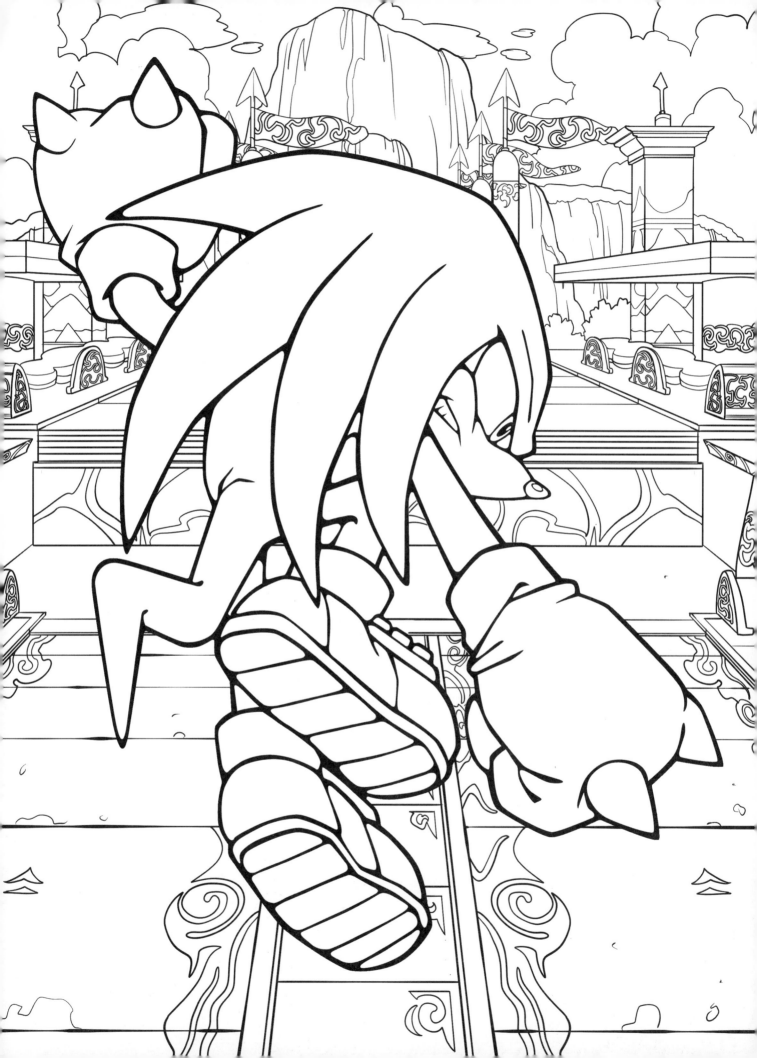

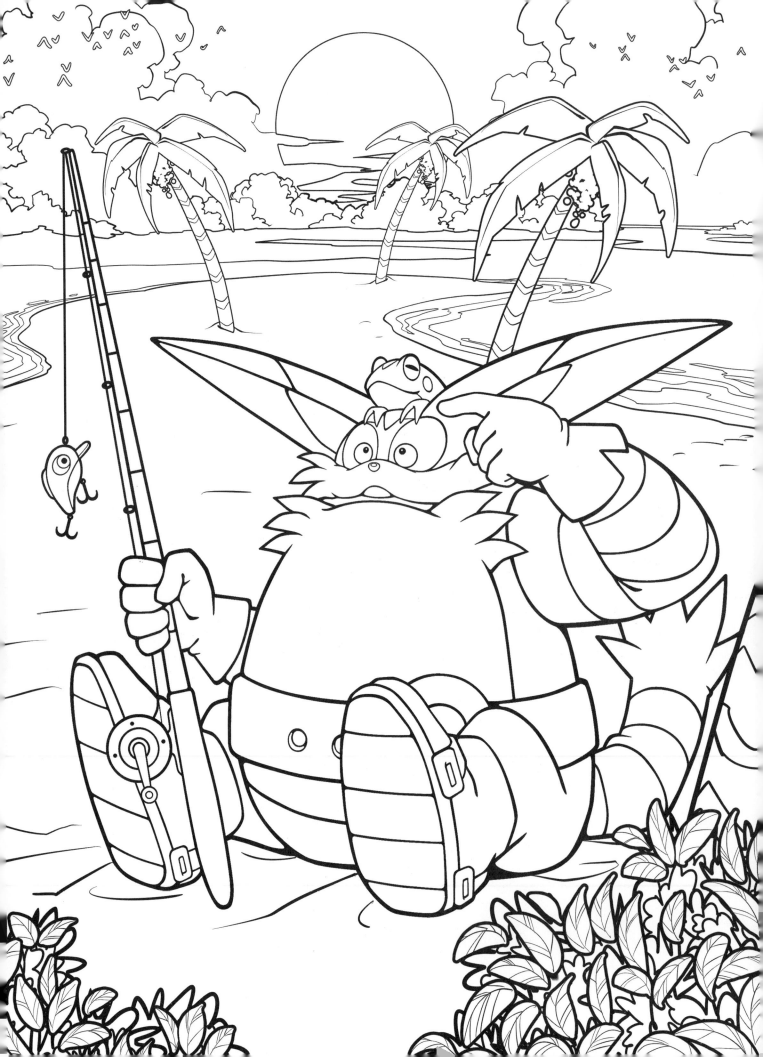

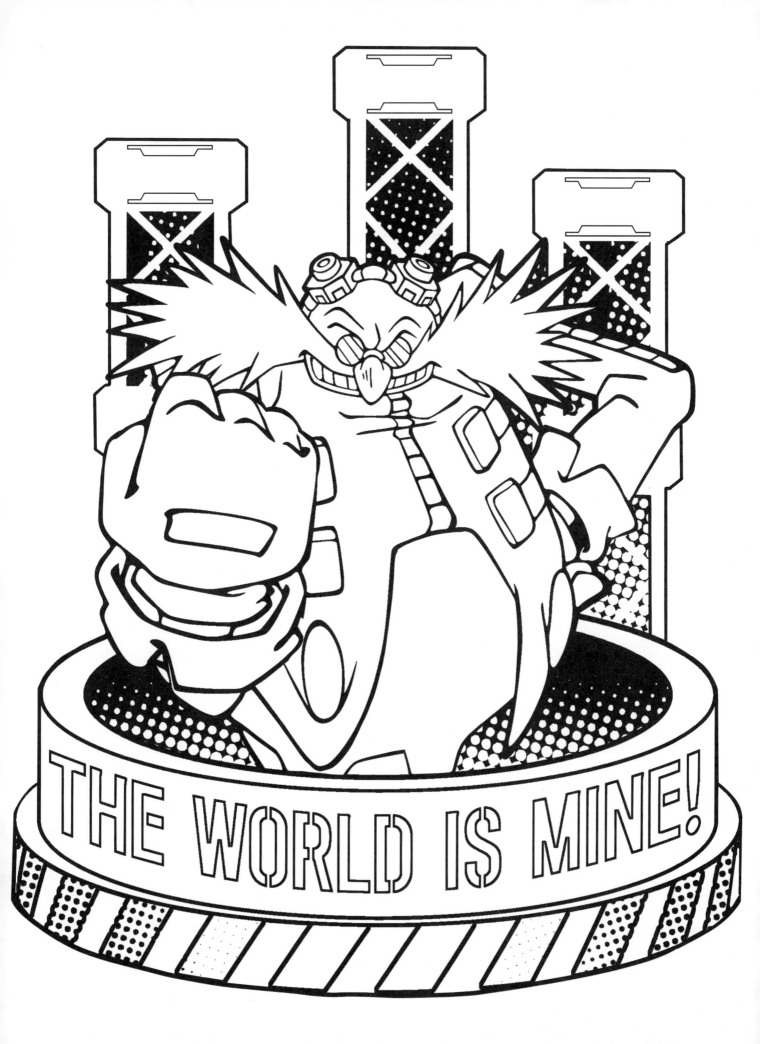

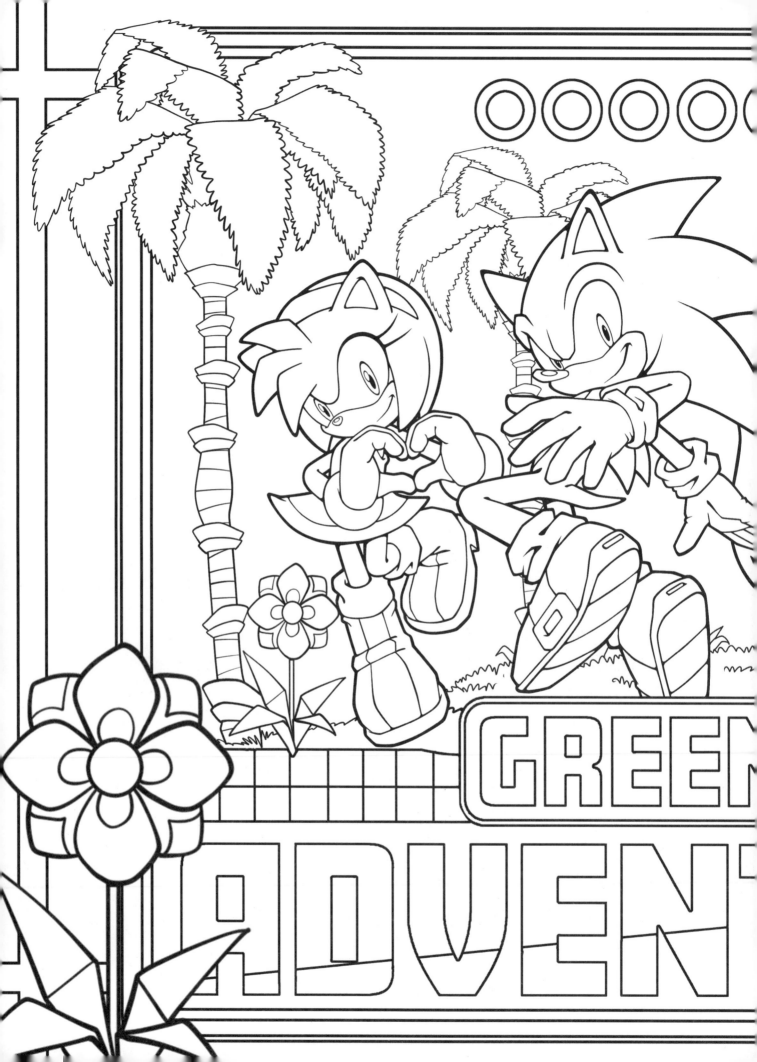

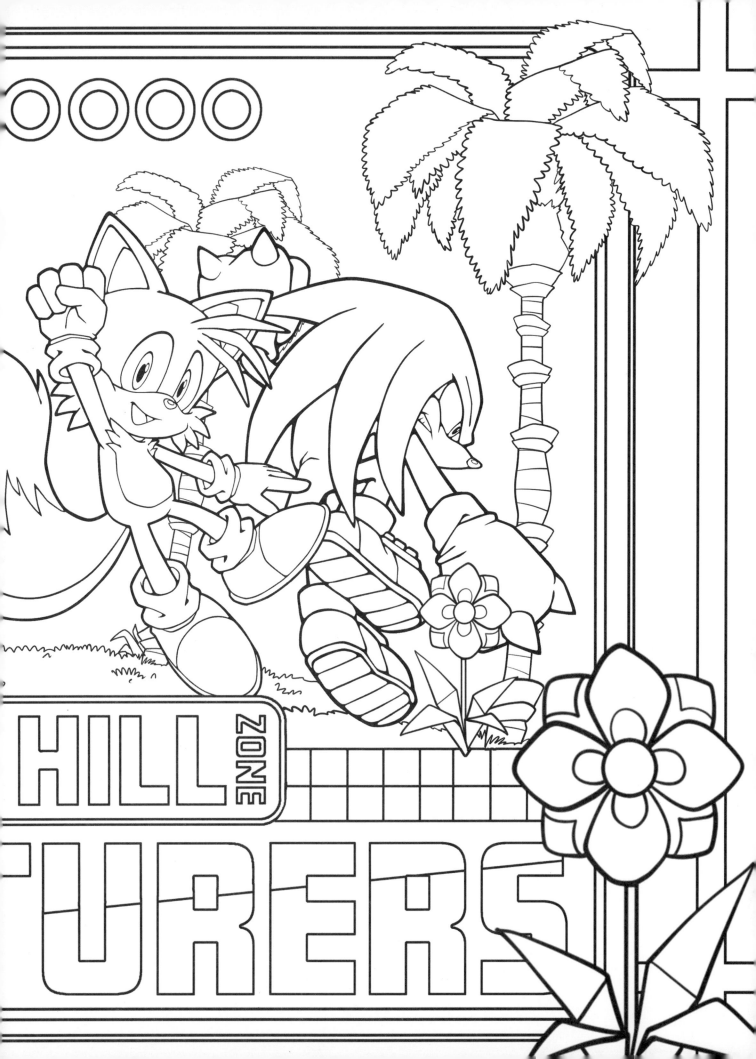

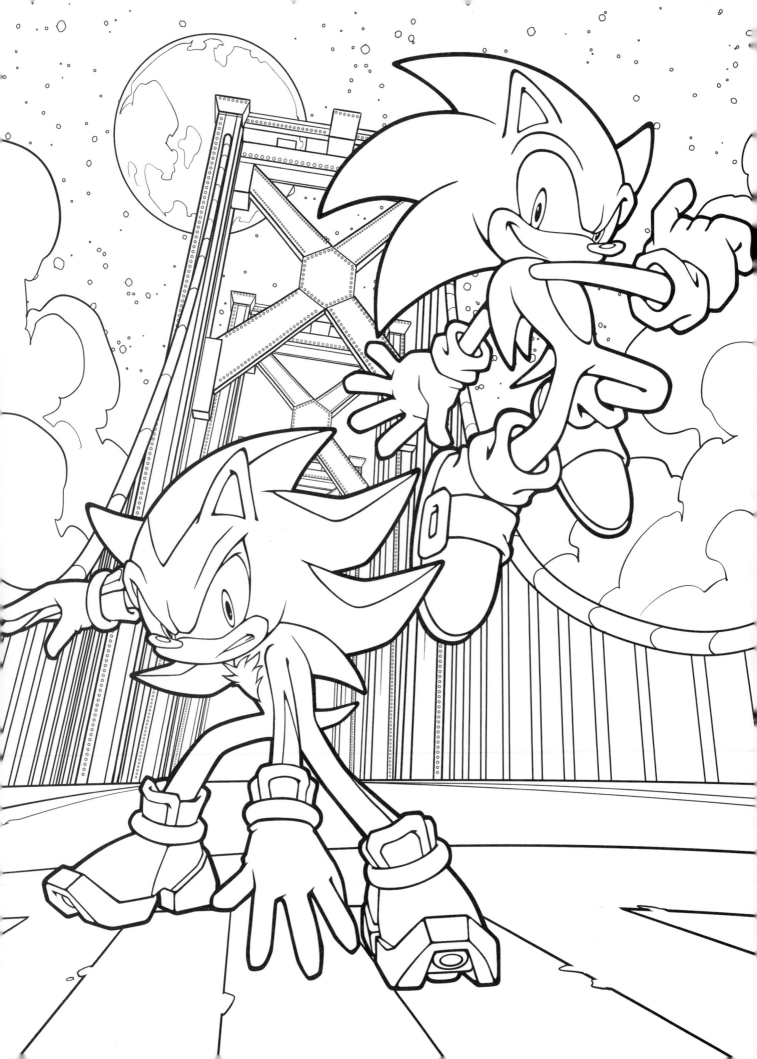

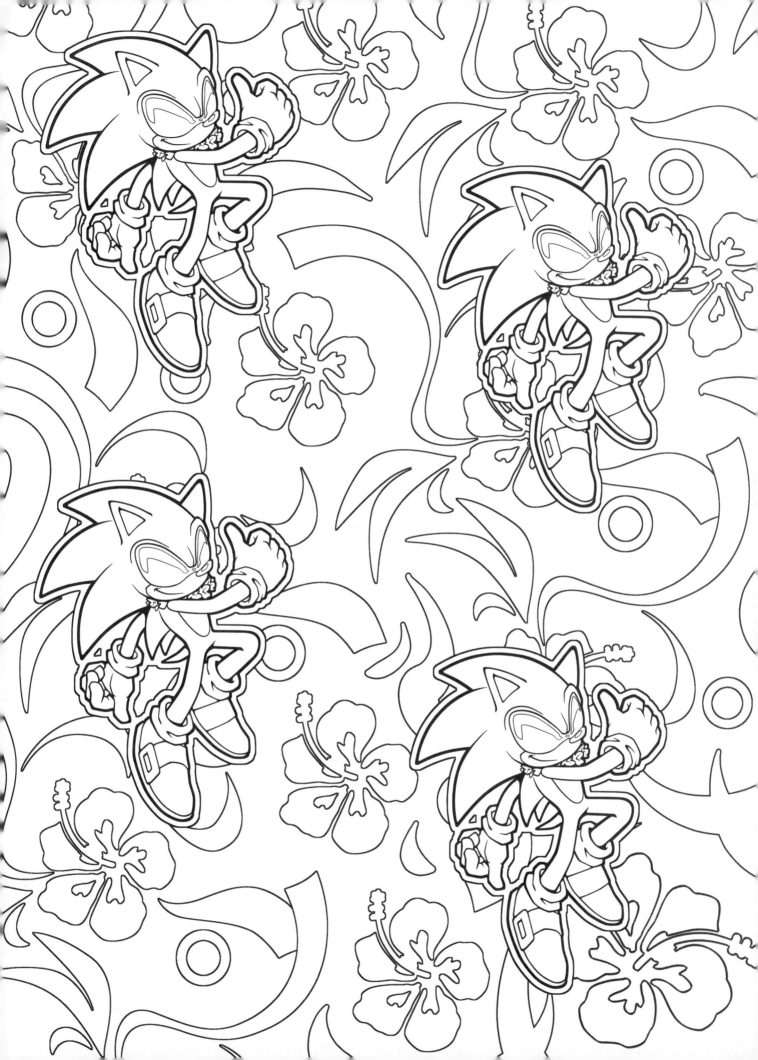

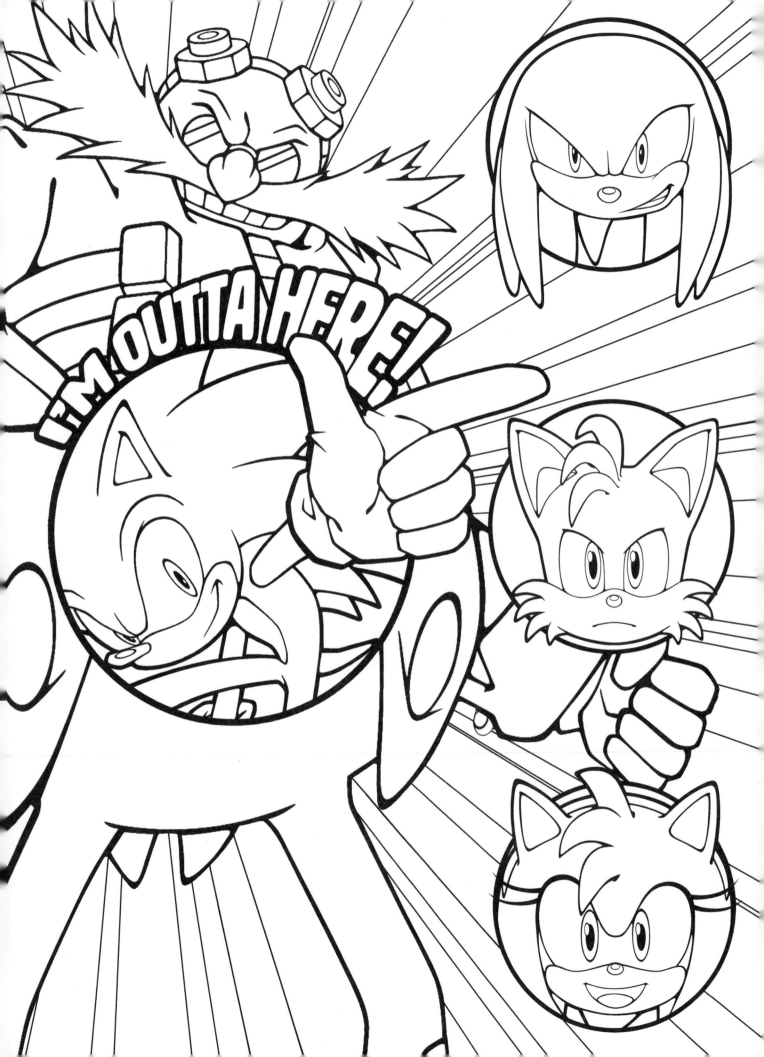

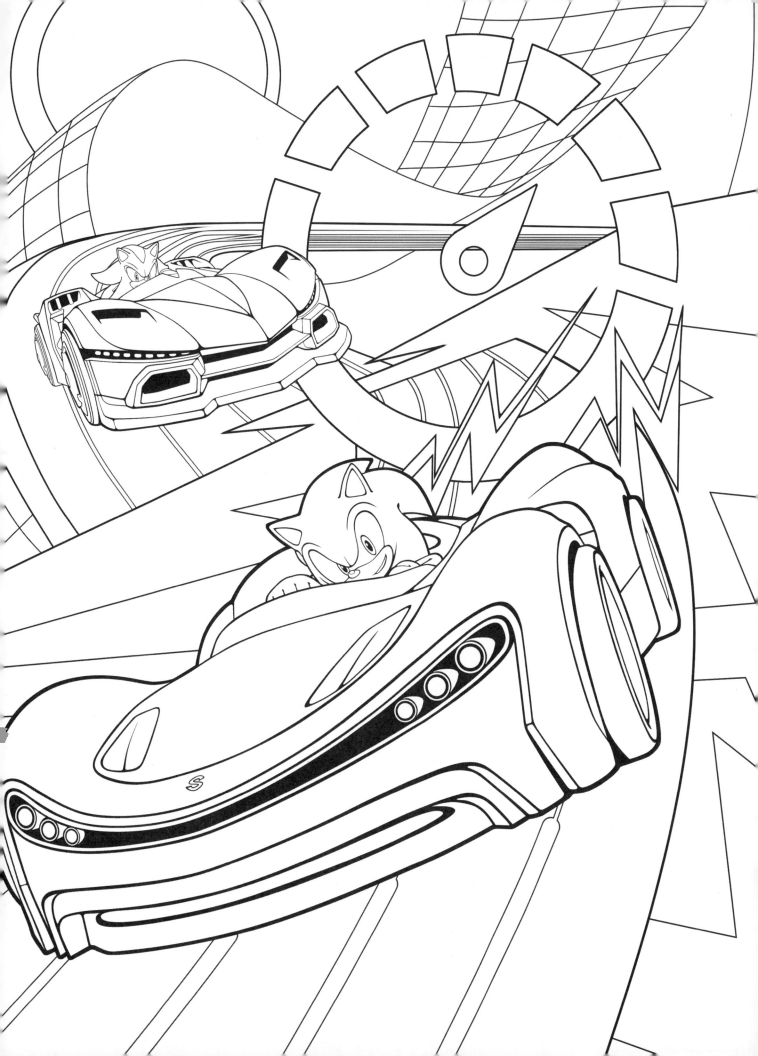

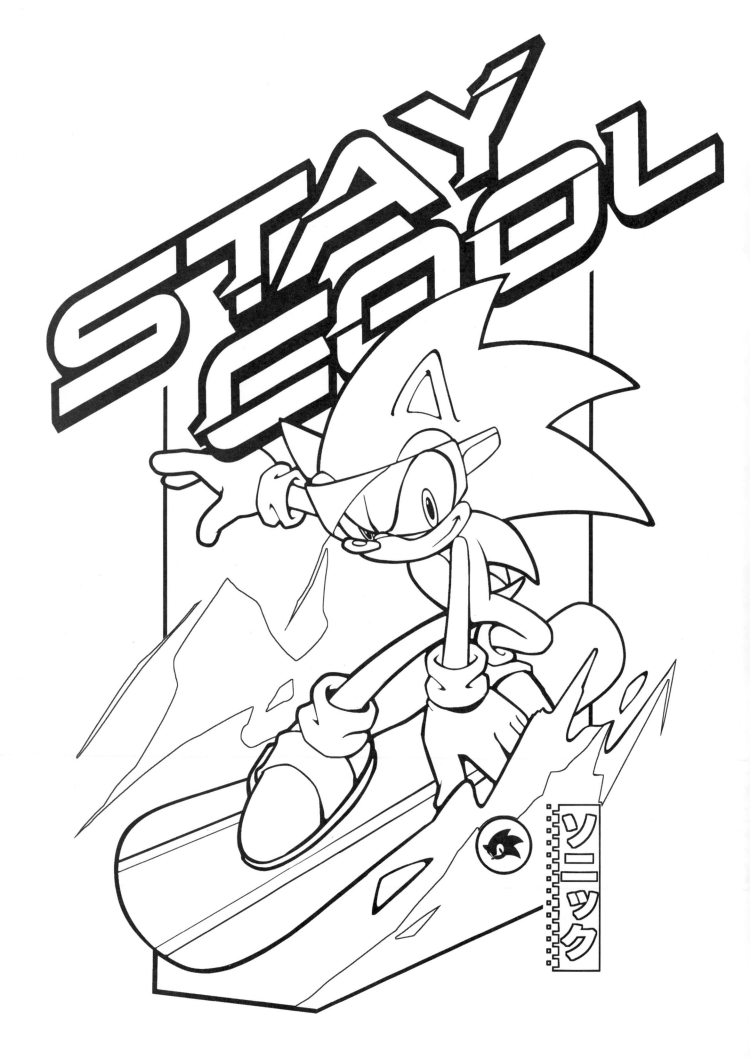

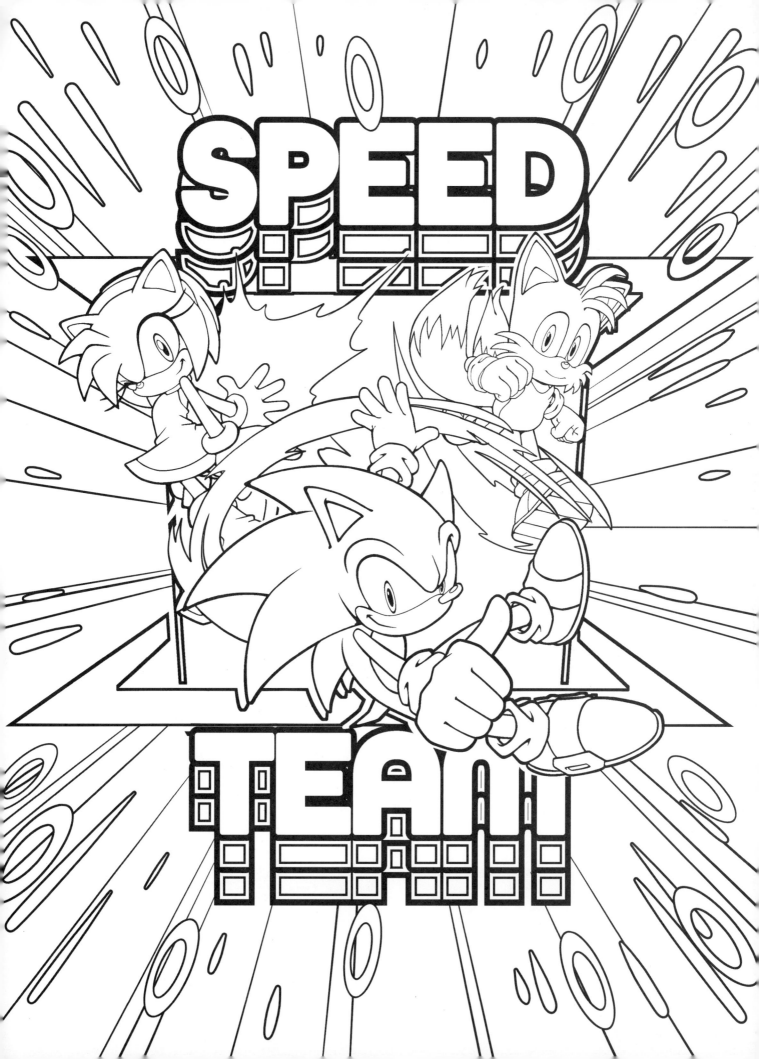

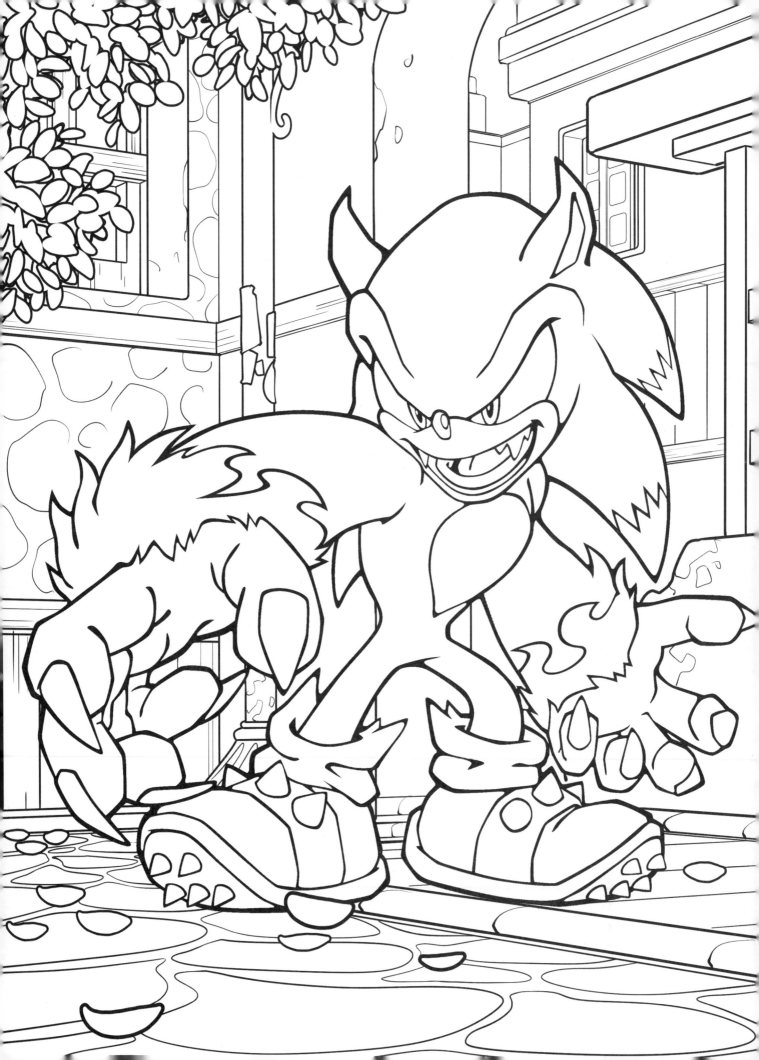

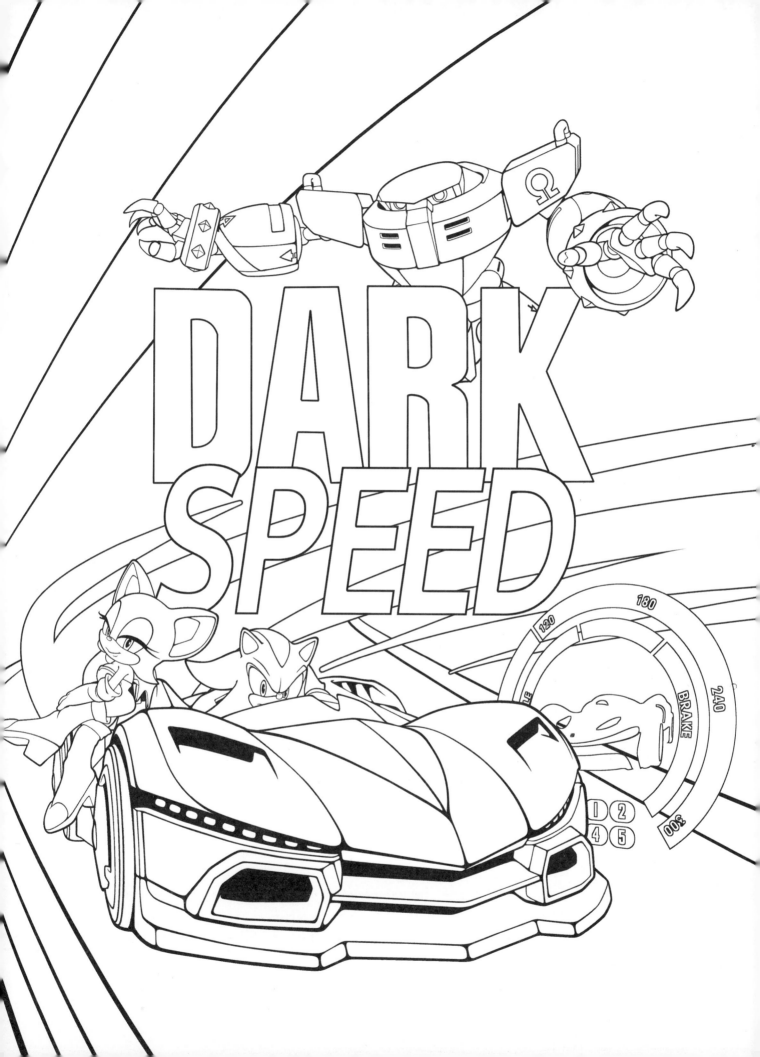

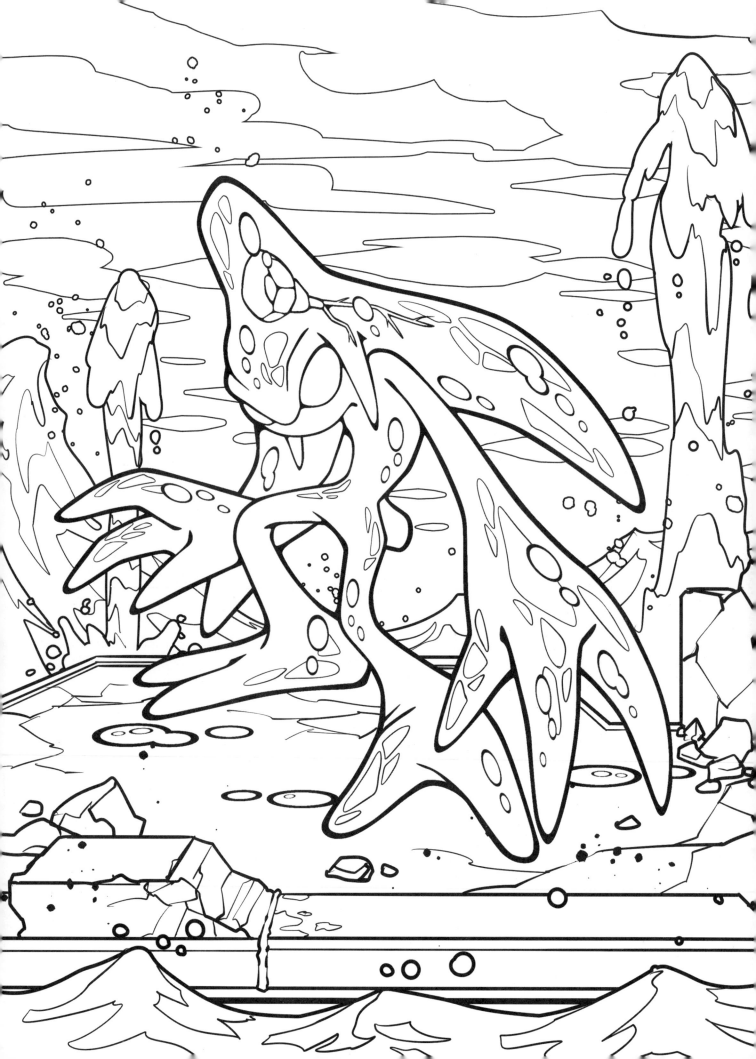

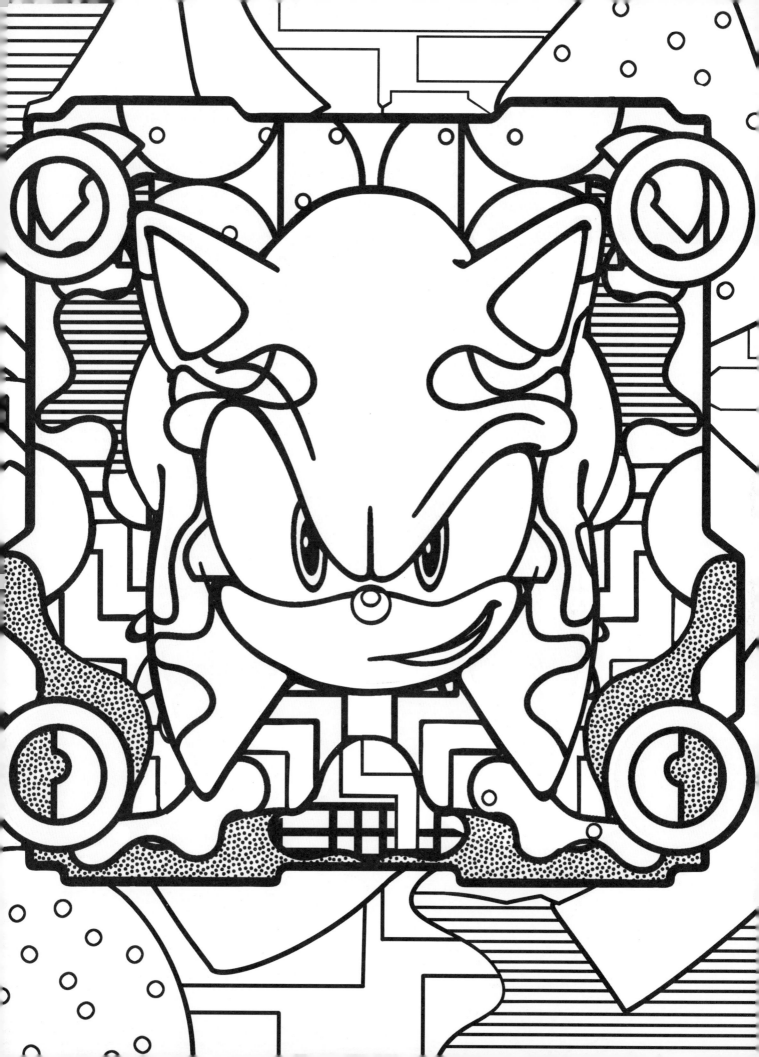

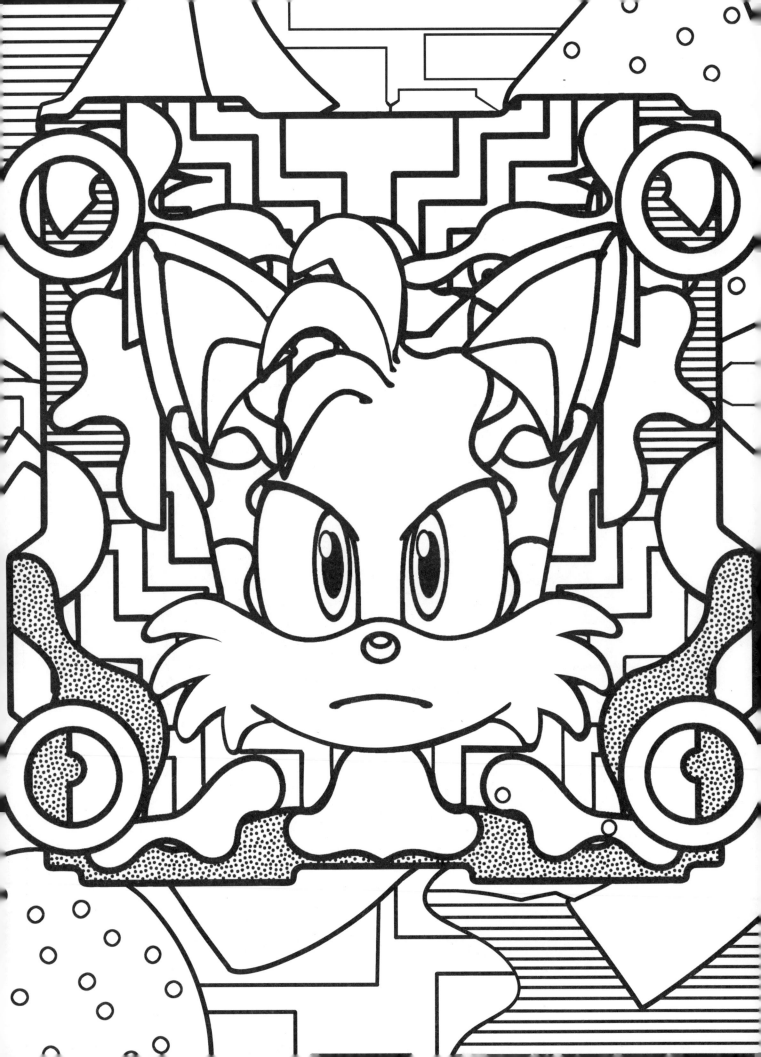

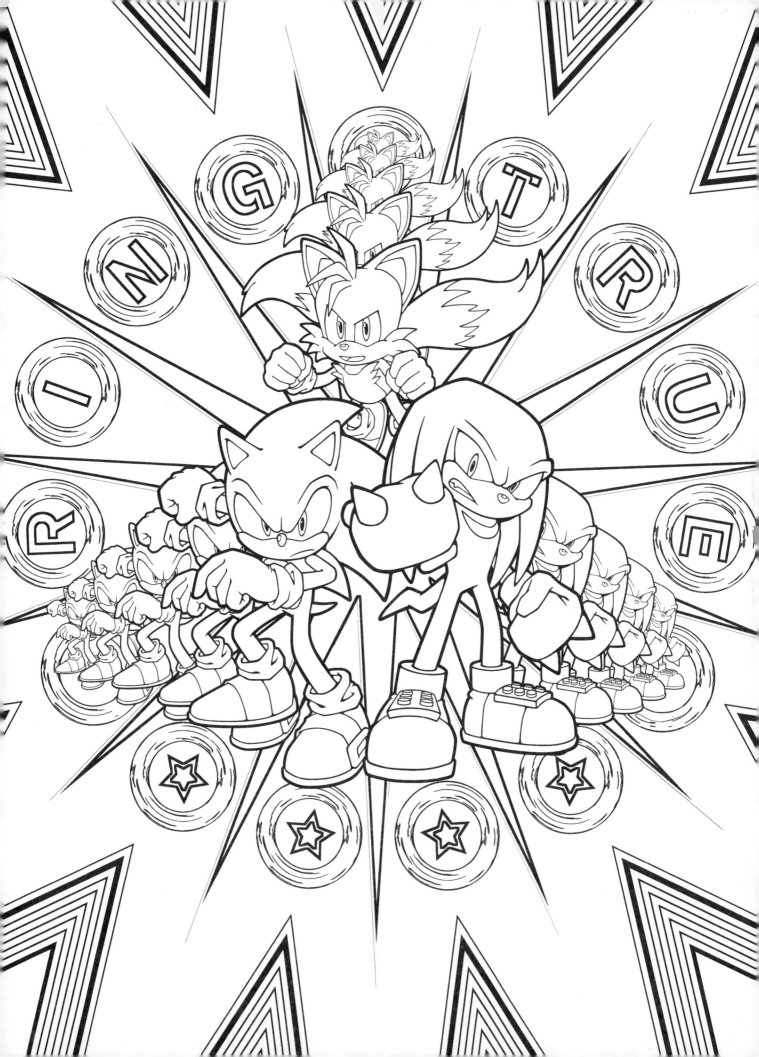

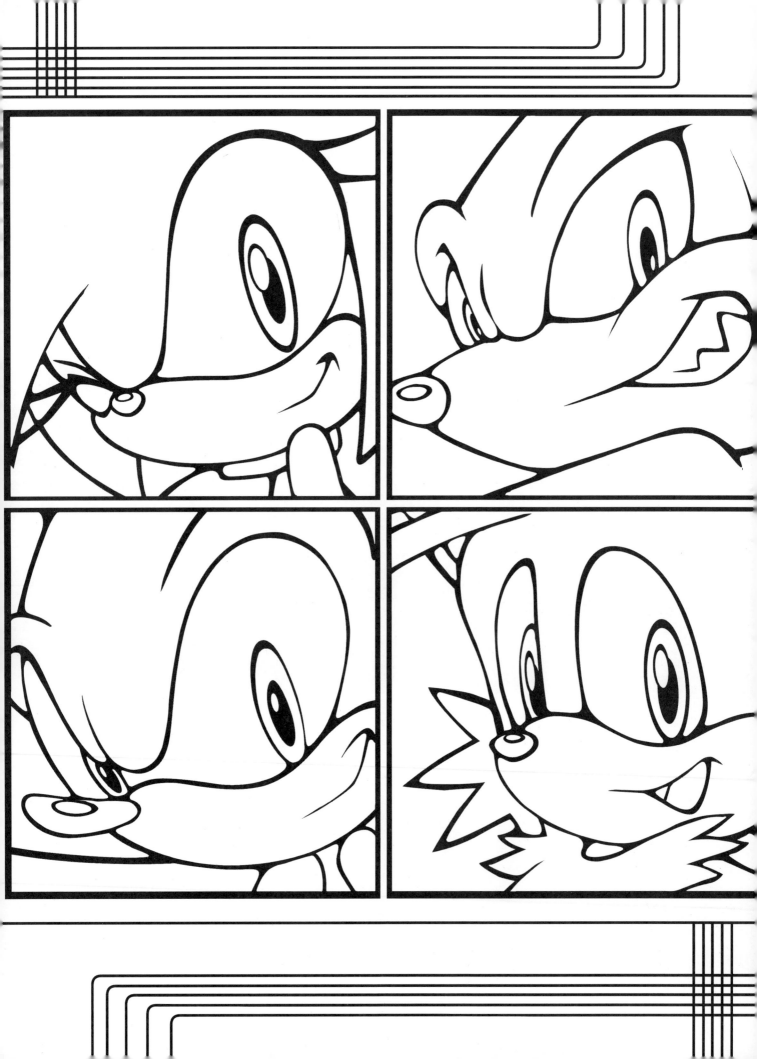

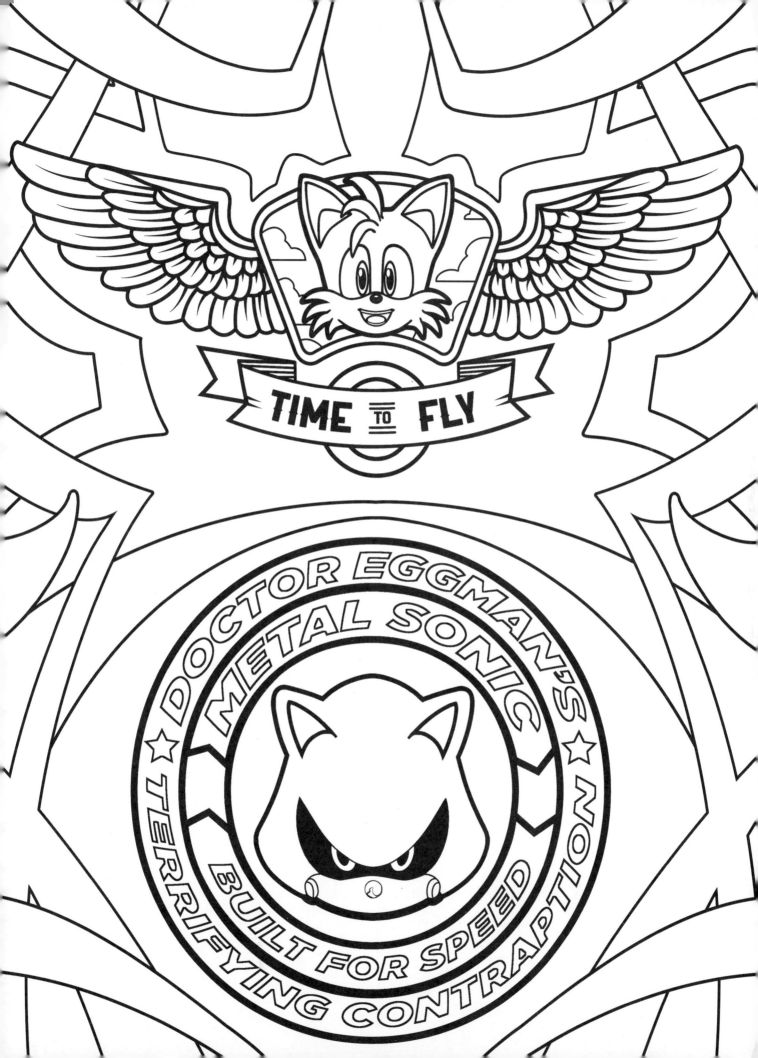

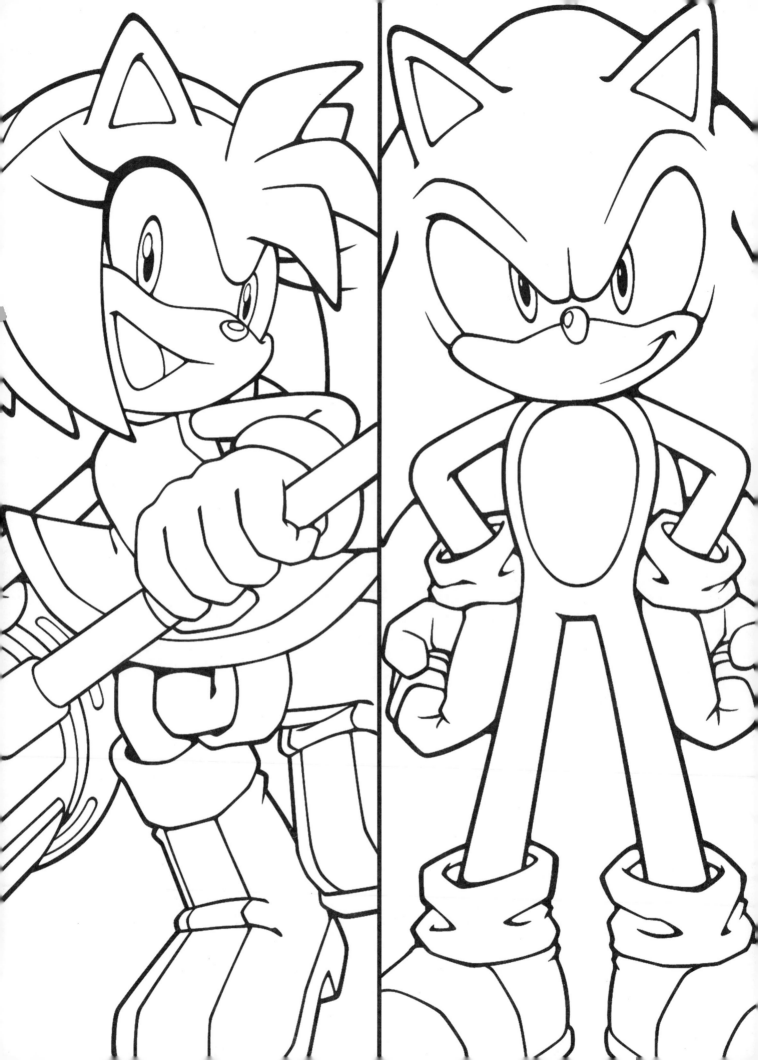

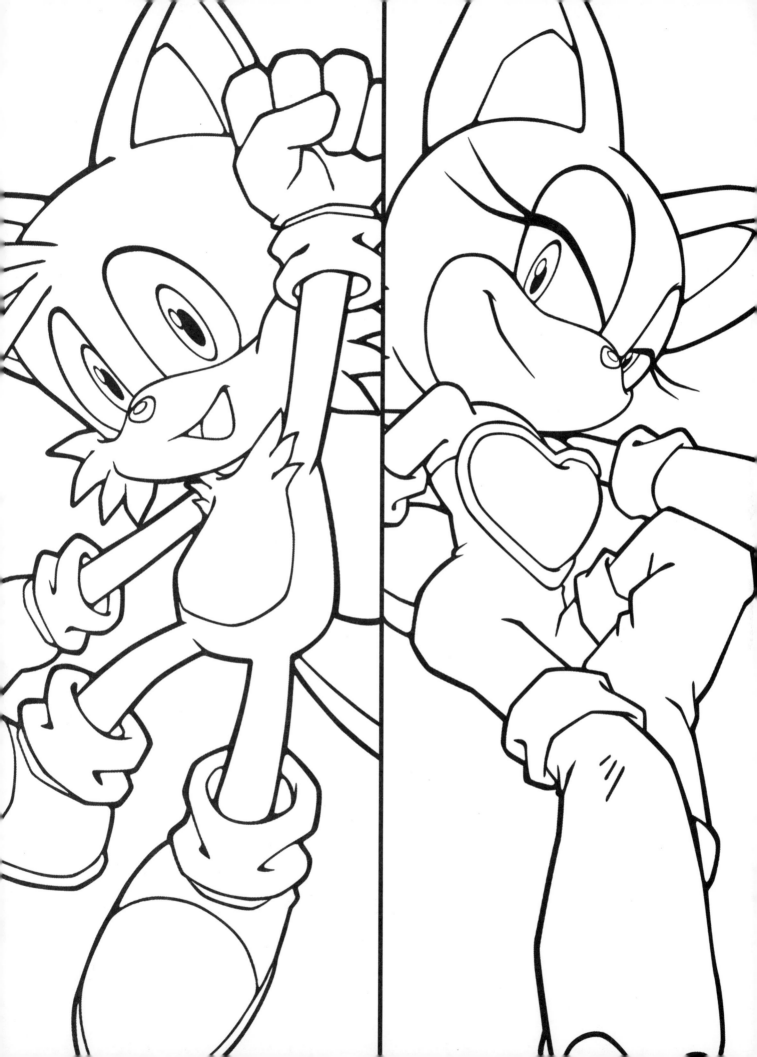

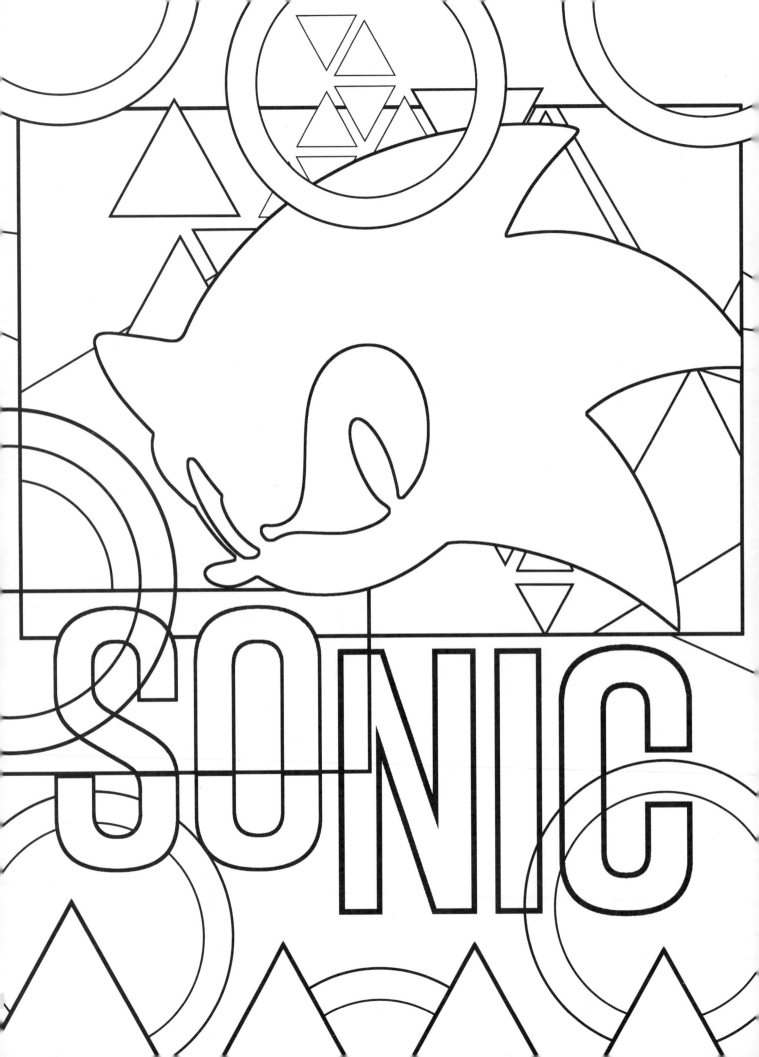

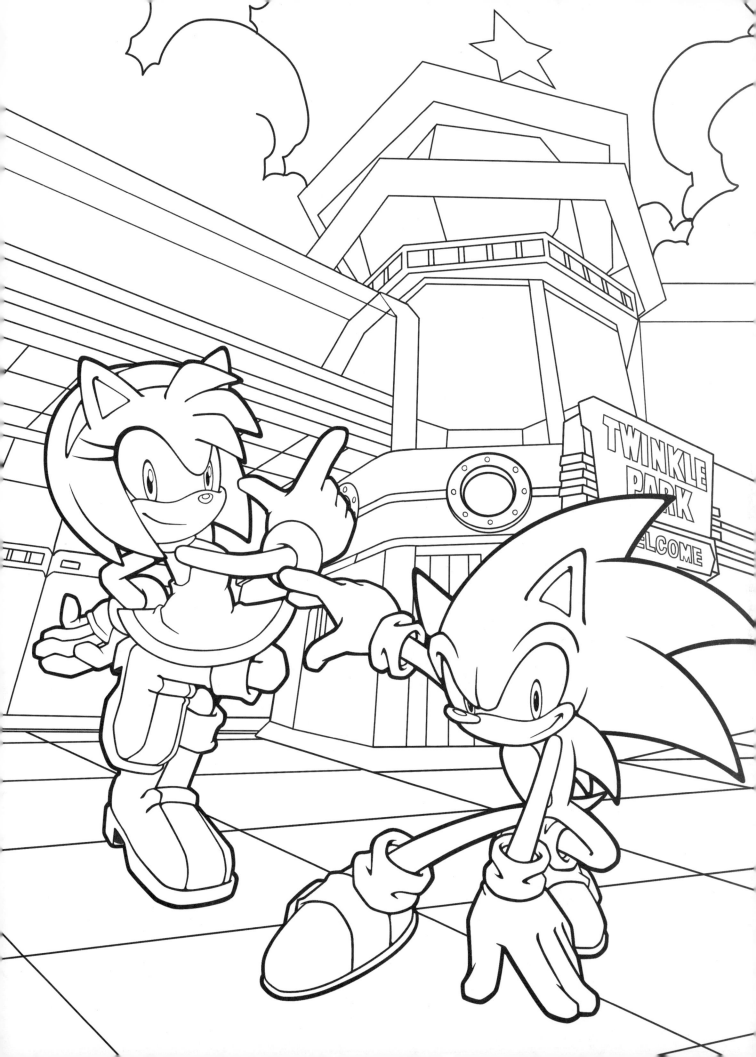

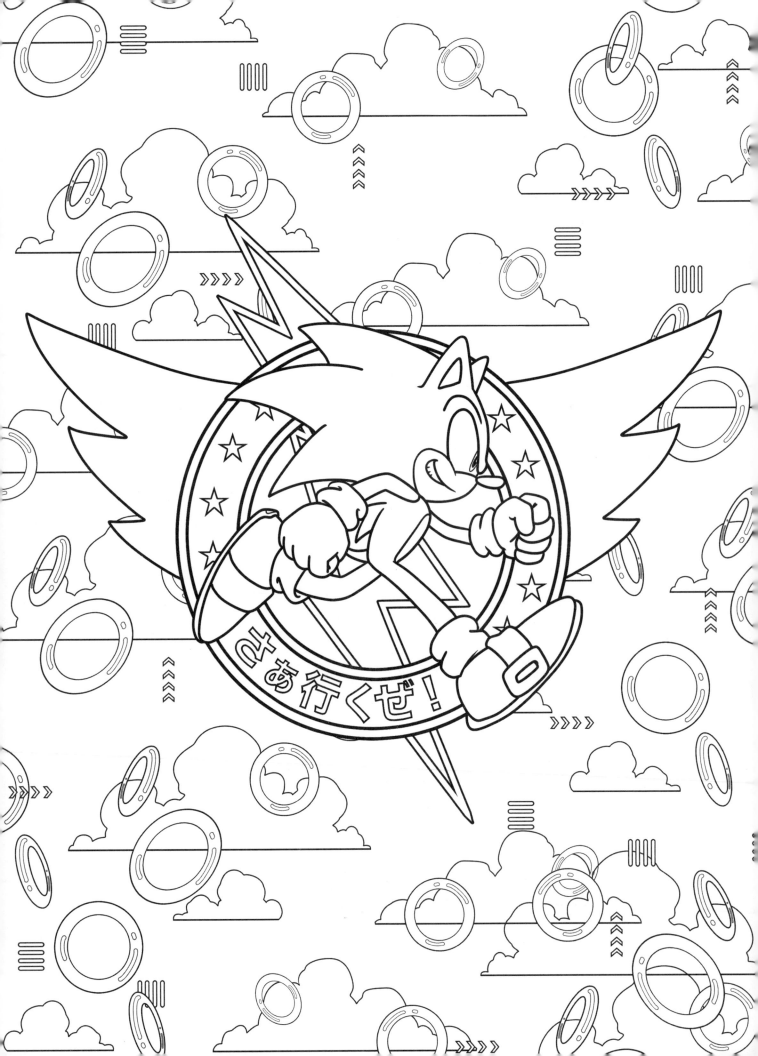

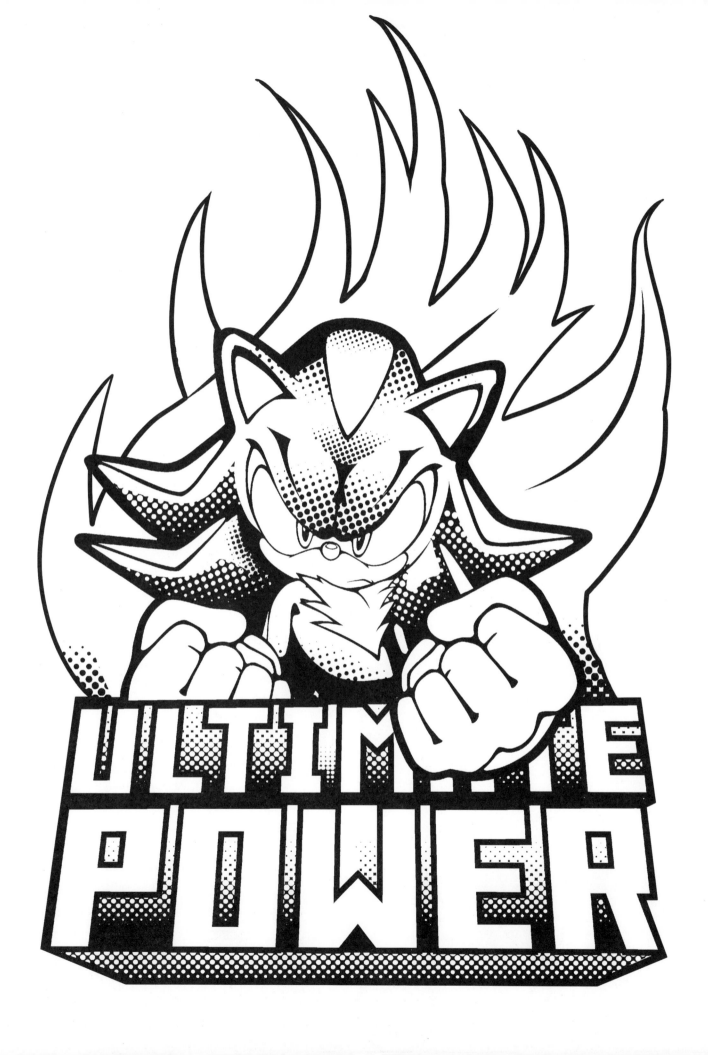

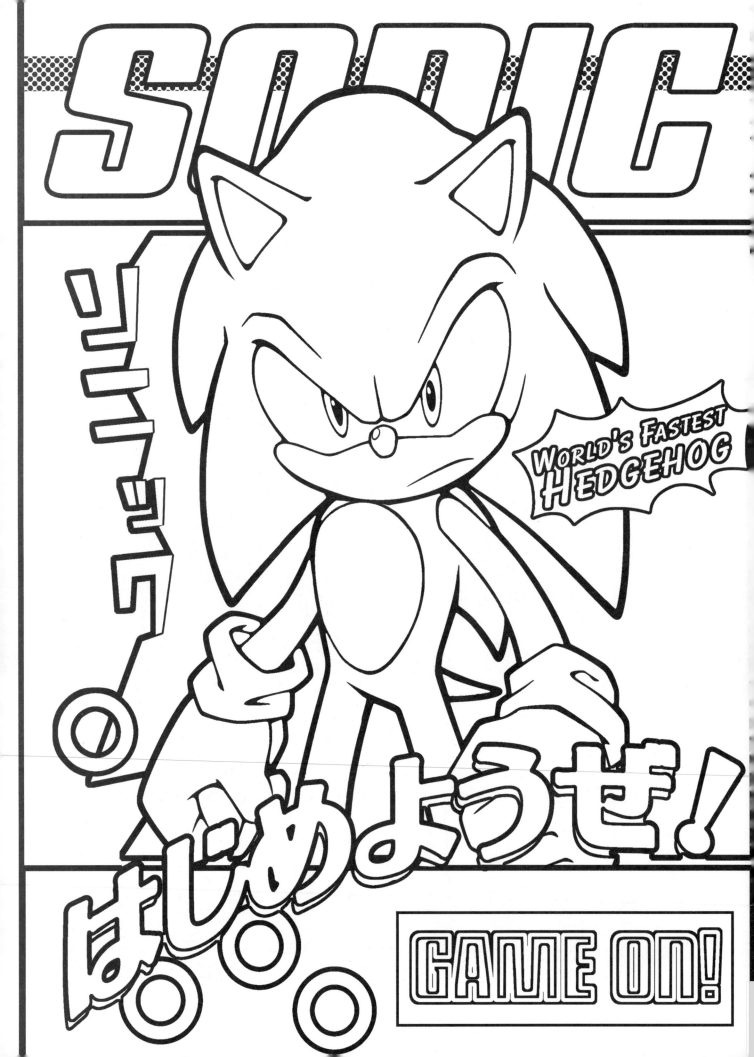

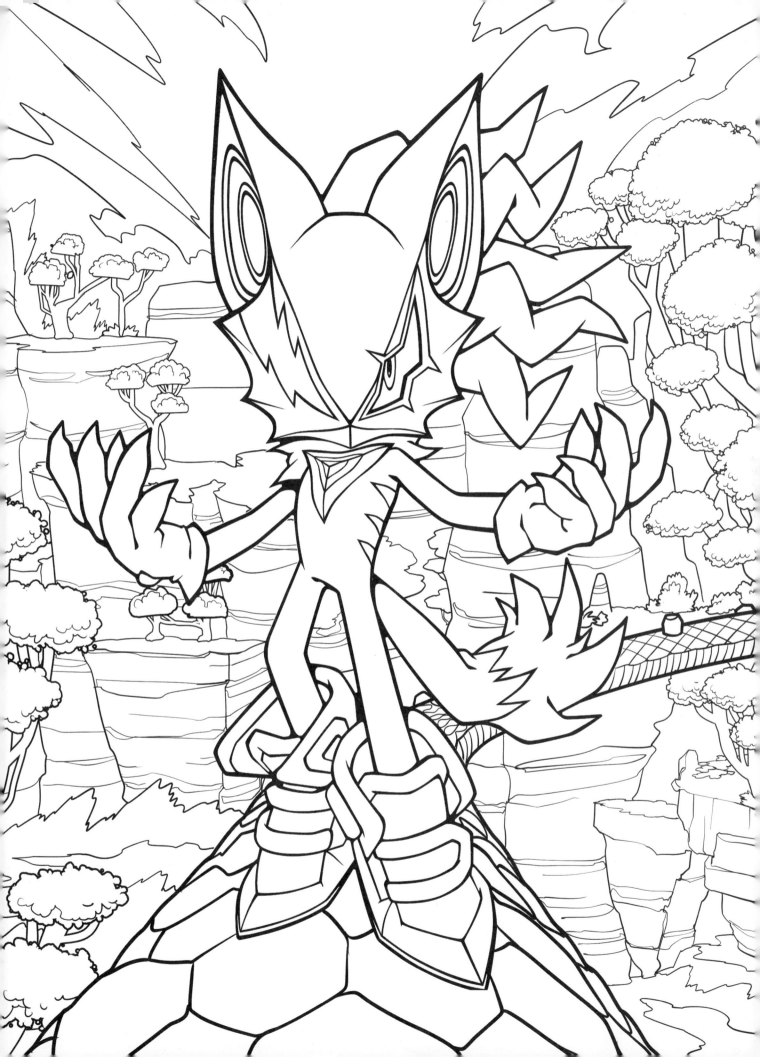

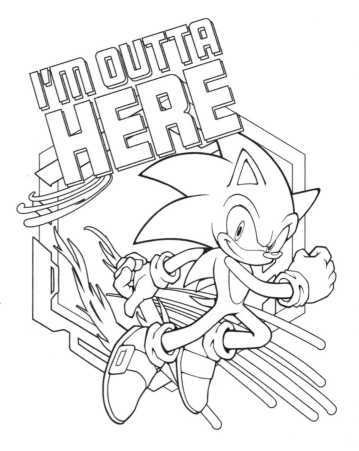

INSIGHT EDITIONS

PO Box 3088
San Rafael, CA 94912
www.insighteditions.com

f Find us on Facebook: www.facebook.com/InsightEditions
🐦 Follow us on Twitter: @insighteditions

ISBN: 978-1-64722-900-9

Publisher: Raoul Goff
VP of Licensing and Partnerships: Vanessa Lopez
VP of Creative: Chrissy Kwasnik
VP of Manufacturing: Alix Nicholaeff
VP, Editorial Director: Vicki Jaeger
Design Manager: Megan Sinead Harris
Editor: Anna Wostenberg
Managing Editor: Maria Spano
Senior Production Editor: Katie Rokakis
Editorial Assistant: Emma Merwin
Production Associate: Tiffani Patterson
Senior Production Manager, Subsidiary Rights: Lina s Palma-Temena

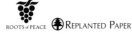

ROOTS of PEACE   🌳 REPLANTED PAPER

Insight Editions, in association with Roots of Peace, will plant two trees for each tree used in the manufacturing of this book. Roots of Peace is an internationally renowned humanitarian organization dedicated to eradicating land mines worldwide and converting war-torn lands into productive farms and wildlife habitats. Roots of Peace will plant two million fruit and nut trees in Afghanistan and provide farmers there with the skills and support necessary for sustainable land use.

Manufactured in China by Insight Editions

10 9 8 7 6 5 4